contents

introduction

The beauty of Thai food is in its contrasts: hot, cool, sour, sweet, crunchy, soft – all with a wonderful citrus tang.

The importance of the preparation and cooking of food in Thailand is one of the first things you notice on arrival there. Everyone appreciates good food and there are restaurants and food stalls everywhere you look. Thailand's tropical monsoon climate is responsible for the superabundance of fruit and vegetables, which includes varieties of everything we grow in the West and at least fifty per cent more. Its physical location has meant that there have been many outside influences on the language, culture, politics, religion and cuisine. In all these areas the Thais have taken what they wanted and discarded the rest, achieving a unique style of their own.

Farming is carried on in the traditional manner and fruit and vegetables are usually organically grown, mostly on smallholdings, and brought to market every day. They do not look as perfect as the produce we can buy here, but what they lack in looks is more than made up for by their flavour and freshness. Eggs are free-range, and delicious too. Thailand is a very fertile country – the combination of monsoon rains and intermittent hot sunshine that occurs during certain months produces lush growth. The flood waters that cover the central 'rice bowl', leaving a thick rich mud in their wake, enable two rice harvests each year, although the second crop is of a slightly poorer quality than the first.

Healthy eating

The Thai diet is very healthy. Even those people who eat meat and fish only eat them in very small amounts. Thai cookery involves the use of several fruit and vegetables that are not regularly used in the West, but which offer a surprising range of nutrients. Limes are a good source of vitamin C, and bean sprouts continue to grow and form nutrients after picking, unlike most other vegetables. A normal helping of mung bean sprouts provides about 75 per cent of the adult RDA of vitamin C, and is also a good source of some of the B vitamins. Garlic helps to lower cholesterol and blood pressure levels. It also has antiviral and antibacterial properties. Papaya is not only a good source of vitamin C and betacarotene, but provides small amounts of calcium and iron too. The juice contains papain, an enzyme similar to pepsin, which is produced by our digestive systems to break down proteins. It is very good for digestive disorders; indeed the food industry uses papain as a natural meat tenderizer.

Over the last few years there has been a huge increase in healthy eating. We have become aware of the enormous problems that arise because of increased production by farmers, and more and more people want to eat free-range eggs rather than battery eggs, 'real' rather than processed cheese, and organically grown vegetables. We are also now aware of problems with pesticides, with nitrates in the water table and with our water supplies in general. We have begun to buy 'green'

cleaning materials and washing powders, we recycle paper and bottles, and we all want to live a life that is better for us and better for our planet. This inevitably means that we have to spend more, but whereas using green products makes us feel we are trying, the pleasure of tasting 'real' food is an instant one. Cooking and eating Thai food is a delicious and unusual way of eating healthily. In a 1991 survey of 1,450 travel agents from twenty-six countries, Thailand's cuisine was rated fourth, after France, Italy and Hong Kong. It has really taken its place in the world.

Ingredients

As Thai cuisine has gained in popularity outside Thailand, first oriental food shops, then supermarkets, and now even many corner shops, sell more and more Thai ingredients, thereby enabling us all to learn to cook Thai-style. Most of the ingredients used in this book are readily available in this country; but I have tried to give alternatives for the more unusual ingredients wherever possible. Remember that it is worth paying a little extra for your ingredients to make sure they taste as good as they should. I would recommend a trip to a good oriental food shop where you will be able to buy all your staples in one go. Vegetarian fish sauce will not be found easily, except in an oriental food shop or possibly a good vegetarian shop that has an oriental section. Similarly, seaweed is available from oriental and vegetarian shops and some large supermarkets, but you are unlikely to find it elsewhere.

Thailand is not the largest rice producer in the world, but it is generally considered to produce the best quality rice, and the dual aspect of quality and quantity have led to it becoming the world's largest exporter of rice. Thai fragrant or jasmine rice is more expensive to buy than other long-grain rice, but it is so delicious that it is well worth paying extra for it. If you cook a lot of oriental food, it is worth taking a trip to an oriental food shop and buying a 3.5 kg/7 lb or 7 kg/14 lb sack of rice, as this is the most economical way of buying it. The rice will keep for a year or more.

Thai food is often very, very hot: chillies are an essential ingredient. In fact, chillies were introduced into Thailand in the sixteenth century, when the Thais craved a hotter spice than the black pepper they used until then. As a general rule, the smaller the chilli, the more fiery the taste. The hottest part of the chilli is the seeds, which you can remove if you wish. I love really hot food, so I don't remove the seeds, and I rarely say to do so in my recipes, but the choice is yours if you prefer your food to be milder. I have generally specified amounts of chilli to produce medium-hot dishes, but you can adjust the amount used to your own taste, just as you can vary the vegetables used in the recipes. Whether you remove the seeds or not, always be very careful when dealing with chillies: don't put your fingers near your eyes, nose or mouth, until you have thoroughly washed your hands and under your nails, and don't let your children get too near them. You

vegetarian thai

vegetari

Jackum Brown

photography by Sandra Lane

hamlyn

Publishing Director: Laura Bamford

Senior Editor: Sasha Judelson
Editor: Jeni Wright
Assistant Editor: Sarah Ford

Art Director: Keith Martin
Senior Designer: Louise Griffiths

Photographer: Sandra Lane
Home Economist: Oona Van den Berg
Stylist: Clare Hunt
Indexer: Hilary Bird

Production Controller: Julie Hadingham

Notes

All dishes serve 4 people, when served as part of a Thai meal.

Standard level spoon measurements are used in all recipes.
1 tablespoon = one 15 ml spoon
1 teaspoon = one 5 ml spoon

Both imperial and metric measurements have been given in all recipes.
Use one set of measurements only and not a mixture of both.

Eggs should be large (sizes 2 and 3) unless otherwise stated. Small eggs are sizes 6 and 7,
medium eggs are sizes 4 and 5 and very large eggs are sizes 0 and 1.

Milk should be full fat unless otherwise stated.

Pepper should be freshly ground unless otherwise stated.

Fresh herbs should be used unless otherwise stated. If unavailable use dried herbs as an
alternative but halve the quantities stated.

Ovens should be preheated to the specified temperature – if using a fan assisted oven,
follow the manufacturer's instructions for adjusting the time and temperature.

Thai cooks rarely deseed chillies (the seeds and surrounding membrane are the hottest part).
If you prefer a milder flavour, remove the seeds before use.

Vegetarian Thai
Jackum Brown

First published in Great Britain in 1998 by Hamlyn
a division of Octopus Publishing GroupLimited
2–4 Heron Quays, London E14 4JP

This paperback edition first published in 2002

Copyright © 1998, 2002 Octopus Publishing Group Limited

British Library Cataloguing-in-Publication Data
A catalogue record for this book is available from the British Library

ISBN 0 600 60714 3

Printed in Hong Kong

Acknowledgements

This book was written thanks to a number of friends. In particular, Khun Bao and Khun Tik of the Kay-Yer Restaurant in Saphankwai, Bangkok,
whom I thank for their patience and expertise; Simon Foord, who generously lent me his apartment in Bangkok; Tom Sexton, who gave hours of
his time helping me create recipes and acting as interpreter; Leslie Smolin and Jean-François Raymond, for the use of their computers in Bangkok
and Suffolk; and Gabrielle Mander, for persuading me to do it. Finally, I want to thank David Brown, for his total support and tasting abilities, and my
family, from whom I learned to love good food.

can become accustomed to the use of chillies quite quickly. A tolerance to their heat builds up, and you notice that they stimulate the appetite and lower the body temperature. Eventually you will realize that you have become an addict, and will want to cook spicy food all the time!

Equipment

Thai kitchens are extremely simple compared to our Western kitchens, so you will already have most of the equipment required to cook Thai food. You will need a wok, I would recommend one with a wooden handle, although you could use a large frying pan at a push. The advantage of the wok is the way the whole surface heats up, the hottest part being in the middle, allowing you to push things to the sides if you think they are almost done and to cook something else in the middle. Woks are deep enough to hold plenty of liquid, so you can cook curries and deep-fry in them, as well as stir-fry.

Thai food is cooked fast. The ingredients are chopped into small pieces before you start, and cooked for a short time over a fairly high heat. They should all be slightly crunchy when they reach your mouth. Thai cooks work on a very high flame, very fast, and lift the wok off the flame when they want to lower the temperature. When you first try cooking in a wok, a medium-high temperature will do; it will enable you to concentrate on the cooking and not waste precious moments adjusting the heat. You have to think fairly carefully about exactly what it is you are cooking, and put the more solid vegetables, such as carrots and broccoli stalks, into the wok first, with the most delicate vegetables, such as small leaves or bean sprouts, going in last, just for a few seconds.

A steamer is also a good idea, although you can rig up your own steamer easily enough by putting a metal colander over a saucepan of boiling water. In this way you can cook rice, if you don't have an electric rice steamer, or you can steam dumplings on a plate placed in the colander with a lid on top to trap the steam.

A mortar and pestle will produce the authentic Thai texture for curry pastes and salads, but you can also use an electric blender or food processor to good effect; indeed, many urban Thais use them these days. If you want to grind fresh whole spices but don't have a mortar and pestle, you can use an electric coffee grinder, well cleaned both before and after use. If you are going to grind fresh spices regularly, it would be worthwhile buying either a mortar and pestle or a coffee grinder to be used only for this purpose.

A heavy kitchen cleaver is useful for peeling, using the blade held horizontally, or for chopping vegetables, opening pineapples and coconuts and finely chopping herbs when you can use the whole blade. Of course, you can also use kitchen knives, vegetable peelers and scissors equally well.

Thai cuisine

Thai eating is usually very relaxed, with six or eight dishes appearing in the centre of the table and everyone helping themselves to a small amount of each. There is always a big bowl of rice, which is so important to Thai people that their verb 'to eat' is literally 'eat rice'. In the northern, mountainous regions of Thailand, people eat a mountain rice, which does not require flooded paddy fields in which to grow. This rice is very poor quality, both in flavour and nutritionally. Glutinous or 'sticky' rice, which is short-grained, is the staple in the rest of northern and northeastern Thailand. The cuisine there is much drier than in the rest of Thailand: people use their fingers to eat with, and make little balls of sticky rice between their fingers and thumb and use them to scoop up the rest of the food. In central and southern Thailand, glutinous rice is mainly used in desserts.

Although Thais like sweet things, and make many dessert-type dishes, they actually eat them as snacks rather than at the end of the meal. I have tried to organize the recipes in this book in a way which is recognizable to most of us, but it is not the true Thai way.

Forks and spoons are the usual implements with which to eat, unless the dish is noodles or a noodle soup, in which case chopsticks and a spoon are used. This use of chopsticks shows the influence of China, which goes back to the first century AD when the tribal T'ai people began to migrate from China down to Burma, Laos, Vietnam and Thailand. Here they joined other tribal people, whose main influences were Burmese and Cambodian, themselves both influenced by India. Over the next few centuries, first one and then another power waxed and waned, then in the thirteenth century the Kingdom of Sukothai was formed. All the tribes absorbed ideas and language from one another and gradually became a cohesive people in their own right. They were called Siamese, and the country became known as Siam. That name was officially changed to Thailand in 1949. All these influences were responsible for what we now know as Thai cuisine, and help to explain how it came to be as immensely varied and unique as it is.

There are not many vegetarian Thais, but their numbers are growing. One of Thailand's greatest sources of foreign exchange is the tourist trade and as significant numbers of tourists are vegetarians it is now becoming quite easy to find wonderful and unusual vegetarian food in Thailand. Specifically vegetarian food stalls exist in many markets, as does the odd vegetarian restaurant. In addition, if you do not see what you want on a menu in a non-vegetarian restaurant, the chef will usually be happy to cook a vegetarian dish for you if you ask.

You will find that the more you try to cook vegetarian Thai food, the quicker and easier it will be, and the more adventurous you will become. I hope you enjoy it as much as I do.

glossary
of ingredients

Above: Bitter Melon;
Opposite from top right: Coriander
Root; and Palm Sugar

Aubergine
Asian aubergines are either long and thin and pink, small and round and pale green, or tiny, round and darker green. They are often available in large supermarkets and Asian and oriental food shops. If you substitute the large purple-black variety more commonly found, remember that they cook faster than the Asian varieties, so adjust your cooking times accordingly.

Banana leaves
These can be found in Asian and oriental food shops, and are used to contain food during steaming and grilling. You can use aluminium foil or small bowls, depending on your needs, but banana leaves are more authentic and they look spectacular. They also impart a faint taste.

Basil
Holy basil is used as commonly as sweet (European) basil in Thai cookery. It has a smaller, darker leaf and purple stalks. It is less sweet than European basil, which may be substituted.

Bean sauce
Black, yellow and red bean sauces made from preserved soya beans are available in jars. Black beans are available in cans and bags and should be rinsed and chopped before use. Unused beans and their liquid can be stored indefinitely if kept in a sealed container in the refrigerator. Bean sauce and beans can be bought from most supermarkets and oriental food shops.

Bitter melon
This has a fairly pale green, lumpy skin and is found in oriental food shops. It has a very bitter taste, but you can substitute marrow, courgette or cucumber if you prefer.

Chillies
There are so many different kinds of chilli it would be impossible to list them all. As a general rule, the smaller the chilli the fiercer the heat, and red chillies are slightly less fierce since they become sweeter as they ripen. Most of the heat of chillies is contained in and around the seeds and the inner membrane. Thai cooks often include the seeds, but you may prefer to remove them for a milder flavour. Fresh orange and yellow chillies are often used in Thai cooking, for their pretty colours as much as anything else. You can occasionally buy them from specialist oriental shops and markets, but otherwise use whatever colour you can get.

Chinese broccoli
This is available fresh at oriental shops. It is quite like European sprouting broccoli except that it is longer and thinner, with more stalk and less floret. The stalk is the most interesting part, and it is sliced and cooked in many different ways.

Coconut milk and cream
These are widely available in cans, packets and blocks (which require added water). You can make coconut milk yourself from desiccated coconut: place 175 g/6 oz coconut in a blender with 300 ml/½ pint hand-hot water; blend for 30 seconds and strain the liquid through muslin, squeezing it as dry as you can. This will produce thick coconut milk. If you return the coconut to the blender and repeat the process, then mix the two extractions, you will get a medium-thick coconut milk, suitable for most dishes. If you put this milk in the refrigerator the 'cream' will rise to the surface and can be taken off. Coconut milk only lasts 1–2 days, even in the refrigerator. If you are using coconut cream, stir it all the time while cooking because it curdles easily.

Coriander
An essential ingredient in Thai cooking. All of this wonderful herb is used – the leaves, stalks and roots. You can store the roots in an airtight container in the refrigerator or in the freezer.

Curry paste
Ready-made pastes are available in jars and packets, or you can make your own (see pages 12–14). They freeze perfectly.

Galangal
This is a root similar to ginger, but the skin is thinner and slightly pink, and the taste is more mellow. It is available in large supermarkets and oriental food shops. It is peeled before use, then either sliced or chopped according to individual recipes. Sliced or chopped galangal can be kept in an airtight container in the refrigerator for up to 2 weeks; it also freezes well. Dried slices are also available, and 1 dried slice is the equivalent of 1 cm/½ inch of the fresh root. Powdered galangal can also be found, but it is not as good.

Ginger
Fresh root ginger is readily available. Use it as galangal, above.

Glutinous rice
A variety of short-grain rice used in many Thai desserts. Sometimes called 'sticky' rice.

Krachai
Also called lesser ginger, this root is smaller and fiercer than ginger and galangal, but it comes from the same family and should be treated in the same way. It is sometimes available fresh from oriental food shops or dried in packets.

Lemon grass
Available from supermarkets in bundles of 4–6 stalks, the straw-like tops should be trimmed as well as the ends, and the stalks thinly sliced. If you can't get fresh lemon grass, dried and powdered lemon grass is also available, or you can use lemon rind or juice as a substitute.

Limes and lime leaves
The variety of lime grown in Thailand is called kaffir. It is slightly different from the ones we normally see, which make a perfectly adequate substitute. Kaffir lime leaves can be bought fresh or dried in oriental food shops and large supermarkets; if unavailable use lime rind or juice, or lemon rind or juice as a last resort.

Mushrooms
Dried black fungus (cloud ear mushrooms) can be found in packets in oriental food shops. They

should be soaked in warm water for 15–20 minutes, then drained before use.

Oyster mushrooms are available fresh from most supermarkets.

Shiitake mushrooms can be found dried in oriental food shops, health food shops and some supermarkets, which also sell them fresh occasionally. If dried, they should be soaked in warm water for 15–20 minutes before use, then the hard stalk cut away and added to the stockpot. Shiitake are expensive, but you only need to use a few at a time.

Straw mushrooms can be found in cans from supermarkets.

Button, chestnut and **field** mushrooms can be used if none of the others are available.

Noodles

There are many different kinds of noodles used in Thai cooking, but the most commonly available are egg noodles, rice vermicelli, rice sticks and glass noodles.

Egg noodles can be bought fresh from oriental shops, but the dried ones, which are widely available at supermarkets, are just as good.

Rice vermicelli are very thin, white and transparent-looking, made from rice as their name suggests. They are dried in long bundles, but can be cut into more convenient lengths with scissors.

Rice sticks are the same as vermicelli, only wider and flatter. They come in varying widths, and it is a matter of personal preference which ones you choose. Occasionally fresh rice sticks can be found in oriental shops; these are white and slippery, and can be cut to any desired width. They do not keep well, and so should be used on the day of purchase.

Glass noodles are also known as cellophane noodles, bean thread noodles and bean vermicelli. They are very like rice vermicelli, but made from mung beans rather than rice.

Oil

Groundnut oil is ideal, although corn oil or other vegetable oils can be used. Do not use olive oil because the taste is too distinctive. After using oil for deep-frying, let it cool, then strain it through a fine sieve or muslin back into the bottle for future use. If you like, you can then keep this oil specially for Thai cooking.

Palm sugar

This soft, raw light-brown sugar is widely used in South-east Asia. In Thailand it is often sold wet, giving it a thick, honey-like consistency, but it is exported in hard blocks that can be broken into pieces and dissolved. It tastes delicious and has a golden colour that is especially attractive in desserts like coconut custard. If you can't get it, use a light muscovado or Indian jaggery sugar.

Papaya

Also called pawpaw, this tropical fruit is available from supermarkets. When unripe, the pale green flesh is used in salads. The orange flesh of ripe papaya tastes best with a little lime juice.

Soy sauce

Light soy sauce is used in the recipes in this

book, except where specified. Dark soy sauce is not only darker in colour, but it is also thicker and slightly sweeter than light soy sauce.

Spring roll wrappers

White and flimsy, these are made from flour and water, and are usually a square shape. Buy them ready-made, fresh or frozen in plastic bags, from oriental supermarkets. They are very fragile, so handle them gently, especially if they have been defrosted. If you can't find the shape of wrapper you need for a recipe, buy whatever you can and cut to the required shape. If spring roll wrappers prove impossible to find, use sheets of filo pastry instead, and cut them to size.

Tamarind water

Dried tamarind pulp can be found in oriental and Indian food shops. Simmer for 2–3 minutes, cool, then squeeze out the juice and discard the pulp and seeds. Tamarind concentrate can be bought in tubs – just dissolve a spoonful in hot water. You can substitute lemon juice.

Tofu

Made from soya beans, tofu is highly nutritious and absorbs other flavours, making it a versatile addition to a vegetarian diet. There are several kinds of tofu available. One of the most useful types is fresh white tofu, which is sold in blocks in its own liquid. It is very delicate and will break up if stirred too much. It does not keep long. Blocks of ready-fried tofu are golden brown on the outside and much more solid. They are ideal for stir-frying. You can buy fairly solid white tofu cakes packed in water in plastic containers; these can be used for stir-frying if you can't get the ready-fried kind. Sheets of tofu, sometimes called 'bean-curd skins', are made from heated soya milk. They are dried, and need to be soaked for 2–3 hours before use. All of these products are available in health food shops, supermarkets and oriental food shops.

Turmeric

This spice is a wonderful colourant with a very mild flavour. Although it can sometimes be found fresh in oriental and Asian food shops, it is most often used in its dried powder form.

Vegetarian fish sauce

Thais use fish sauce in a great many dishes. A vegetarian version can be found sometimes, but only in large oriental food shops. If you cannot get it, substitute light soy sauce or salt.

Vinegar

It is worth looking for white rice vinegar or distilled white vinegar in large supermarkets or oriental shops. If you cannot find them, use cider vinegar. Malt vinegar will not suit oriental food.

Wonton wrappers

Made from flour and eggs, these are deep yellow or brown in colour. They are sold ready-made, fresh or frozen in plastic bags, from oriental food shops. If a recipe uses differently shaped wrappers, cut them to shape with scissors. Otherwise, use sheets of filo pastry and cut them to the required shape.

Several of these basic recipes are for things you can buy already made up, but it is both fun and interesting to know how to make them yourself. Red and green curry pastes are available in jars and tubs from supermarkets and oriental food shops. Vegetable stock can be made from stock cubes. You can dry-fry dried onion and garlic flakes quite successfully if you are in a hurry, and most people have their own favourite method of cooking rice. However, none of the ready-made products tastes quite as good – or gives you as much satisfaction – as if you have made it from scratch at home.

basic *recipes*

Preparation time: 15 minutes

green curry paste

15 small fresh green chillies

4 garlic cloves, halved

2 lemon grass stalks, finely chopped

2 lime leaves, torn

2 shallots, chopped

50 g/2 oz fresh coriander leaves, stalks and roots

2.5 cm/1 inch piece of fresh root ginger, peeled and chopped

2 teaspoons coriander seeds

1 teaspoon black peppercorns

1 teaspoon peeled lime rind

½ teaspoon salt

2 tablespoons groundnut oil

○ Put all the ingredients in a blender or food processor and blend to a thick paste.

○ Alternatively, put the chillies in a mortar and crush with the pestle, then add the garlic and crush it with the chillies, and so on with all the other ingredients, finally mixing in the oil with a spoon.

○ Transfer the paste to an airtight container and store in the refrigerator for up to 3 weeks.

red curry paste

10 large fresh red chillies

2 teaspoons coriander seeds

5 cm/2 inch piece of galangal, peeled and finely chopped

1 lemon grass stalk, finely chopped

4 garlic cloves, halved

1 shallot, roughly chopped

1 teaspoon lime juice

2 tablespoons groundnut oil

○ Put all the ingredients in a blender or food processor and blend to a thick paste.

○ Alternatively, you can pound all the ingredients together with a mortar and pestle.

○ Transfer the paste to an airtight container and store in the refrigerator for up to 3 weeks.

Preparation time: 15 minutes

Preparation time: 15 minutes

yellow curry paste

- Put all the ingredients in a blender or food processor and blend to a thick paste.
- Alternatively, you can pound all the ingredients together with a mortar and pestle.
- Transfer the paste to an airtight container and store in the refrigerator for up to 3 weeks.

3 small fresh yellow or orange chillies
4 garlic cloves, halved
4 shallots, roughly chopped
3 teaspoons turmeric powder
1 teaspoon salt
15 black peppercorns
1 lemon grass stalk, chopped
2.5 cm/1 inch piece of fresh root ginger, peeled and chopped

Preparation time: 15 minutes
Cooking time: 2 minutes

massaman curry paste

3 cardamom pods
1 teaspoon coriander seeds
1 teaspoon cumin seeds
2 cloves
6 small fresh red chillies
2 garlic cloves, halved
1 teaspoon ground cinnamon
1 cm/½ inch piece of fresh root
  ginger, peeled and finely
  chopped
3 shallots, chopped
1 lemon grass stalk, chopped
juice of ½ lime

- Remove the cardamom seeds from their pods and dry-fry them for 2 minutes with the coriander and cumin seeds and the cloves.
- Transfer the dry-fried spices to a blender or food processor and blend with the remaining ingredients to form a thick paste. Alternatively, pound them all with a mortar and pestle.
- Transfer the paste to an airtight container and store in the refrigerator for up to 3 weeks.

panang curry paste

4 shallots, chopped
8 garlic cloves, chopped
10 dried chillies, deseeded
3 lemon grass stalks, chopped
3 coriander roots
2.5 cm/1 inch piece of fresh
  root ginger, peeled and
  chopped
½ teaspoon coriander seeds,
  dry-fried
1 teaspoon cumin seeds,
  dry-fried
2 tablespoons Roasted Peanuts
  (see page 16)
2 tablespoons groundnut oil

- Put all the ingredients in a blender or food processor and blend to a smooth paste.
- Alternatively, you can pound all the ingredients together with a mortar and pestle.
- Transfer the paste to an airtight container and store in the refrigerator for up to 3 weeks.

Preparation time: 20 minutes

Preparation time: 7-8 minutes
Cooking time: 2-2½ minutes

crispy garlic and shallots

Thai people usually flavour their oil with garlic and shallots before using it. The crispy garlic and shallots are drained from the oil, reserved, and then sprinkled on to many different dishes. If you like, you can deep-fry just garlic or shallots, or you can deep-fry them both as here, then store them together rather than separately. It's all a matter of personal choice.

about 750 ml/1¼ pints
    groundnut oil for deep-frying
25 g/1 oz garlic, finely chopped
25 g/1 oz shallots, finely
    chopped

- Heat the oil for deep-frying in a wok. When the oil is good and hot, throw in the garlic and stir for about 40 seconds, watching it sizzle and turn golden.
- Remove the garlic with a slotted spoon, draining as much oil as possible back into the wok, then spread the garlic out to dry on kitchen paper. Repeat the process with the shallots allowing 1½–2 minutes frying time.
- When the garlic and shallots are dried and crispy, you can store them in separate airtight containers, where they will keep for up to 1 month.
- When the groundnut oil is cold, return it to an airtight container, to be re-used.

Preparation time: 2 minutes
Cooking time: 1 minute

crispy basil

You can make Crispy Mint in the same way, using 25 g/1 oz fresh mint leaves.

2 tablespoons groundnut oil
25 g/1 oz fresh basil leaves
1 small fresh red chilli, finely
  sliced

○ Heat the oil in a wok until it is hot, add the basil and chilli and stir-fry for 1 minute until crispy. Remove with a slotted spoon and drain on kitchen paper.

crushed roasted nuts

25 g/1 oz unroasted peanuts
  or cashew nuts

○ Dry-fry the nuts in a frying pan, using no oil. Stir them around constantly until they turn a lovely golden colour. Remove from the heat and allow to cool.
○ Place the nuts in a plastic bag and break into small pieces using a rolling pin.
○ You can roast and crush a larger quantity of nuts, then store what you do not need for up to 1 month in an airtight container in the refrigerator.

Preparation time: 1–2 minutes
Cooking time: 3–5 minutes

ground roast rice

25 g/1 oz uncooked rice

○ Dry-fry the rice in a frying pan, using no oil. Shake and stir it around constantly until it turns a lovely golden colour. Remove from the heat and allow to cool.
○ Grind the rice with a mortar and pestle, or in a clean coffee or spice grinder.
○ If you like, you can make a larger quantity, then store what you do not need immediately. It will keep up to 1 month in an airtight container in the refrigerator.

Preparation time: 1–2 minutes
Cooking time: 3–5 minutes

Preparation time: 5 minutes
Cooking time: 15–20 minutes

rice
kao

There are several different methods of cooking rice. A great many Thais use electric rice steamers these days, but the following recipe has been used by people all over South-east Asia for centuries. I recommend using Thai jasmine or fragrant rice. Although it is more expensive than other long-grain rice, it is superb quality, tastes delicious and is what you would be eating were you in Thailand. I generally cook about 125 g/4 oz rice per person, unless I am cooking several dishes, when I might cook only 50 g/2 oz or 75g/3 oz per person.

500 g/1 lb Thai jasmine or fragrant rice
1.8 litres/4 pints water

○ Rinse the rice several times in a large bowl of water until the water is clear of rice starch. Drain thoroughly.

○ Bring the measured water to the boil in a saucepan and put the rice into it, giving it a stir to ensure that the grains are not stuck together in clumps. Bring back to the boil and cook, stirring occasionally, for 5–6 minutes.

○ Drain the rice into a metal colander and place it over another saucepan of boiling water, making sure that the level of the water is well beneath the rice. Take a chopstick and push it through the rice to the colander, to leave a steam hole. Do this in several places. Place a saucepan lid over the rice in the colander – it should not touch the rice – and steam for about 15 minutes, topping up the water level if necessary.

○ Remove the lid, fluff up the rice a little with a fork and let it steam for 3–4 minutes more. It will now be ready to serve. You can cook your rice in this way, well in advance of your meal, and just leave it covered until 10 minutes before you need it, when you bring the water back to the boil and warm the rice again. You can also 'unfreeze' frozen rice quite fast using this method.

2 large onions, quartered

4 large fresh red chillies

250 g/8 oz carrots, halved

¼ small white cabbage, halved

1 small head of celery (including leaves), chopped

50 g/2 oz fresh coriander leaves, stalks and roots

25 g/1 oz fresh basil leaves and stalks

½ head Chinese leaves, chopped

½ mooli radish, peeled

25 black peppercorns

½ teaspoon salt

1 teaspoon light muscovado sugar

2 litres/3½ pints water

Preparation time: 5–10 minutes
Cooking time: about 1½ hours

vegetable stock

- Put all the ingredients and the water into a large heavy-bottomed saucepan or casserole. Bring to the boil, cover and simmer for 1 hour.
- Remove the lid and boil hard for 10 minutes. Allow to cool, then strain. Freeze any stock you are not using immediately.

Thai people eat very frequently – in fact they eat five or six times a day, usually fairly light meals or 'snacks' every time. People eat whenever they feel hungry, and everywhere you go the streets are lined with stalls selling delicious food that is cooked to order. However, when Thais sit down at home to eat, all the food is brought out at the same time: the concept of a starter or first course does not exist. Snacks just exist in their own right, alongside everything else. I think the dishes in this chapter all work well as starters, party food, or indeed if you serve four or five of them, they make a lovely light lunch or supper.

snacks and *starters*

Makes 12
Preparation time: 15–20 minutes, plus 15–20 minutes soaking
Cooking time: 3–4 minutes each batch

spring rolls
bapia tod

- First make the filling: heat the wok and add the oil, garlic, bean sprouts, cabbage, mushrooms and celery. Stir-fry for 30 seconds, then add sugar, soy sauce and noodles. Stir-fry for 1 minute, then remove from the heat and place the ingredients on a plate. Wipe the wok clean with kitchen paper.
- Put 1 tablespoon of the filling on one corner of a spring roll wrapper, then roll it up, wrapping in the ends to form a neat tube. Use a little oil to stick down the last corner, then secure the roll with a toothpick. Repeat with the remaining wrappers and filling.
- Heat the oil for deep-frying in a wok, pop in a batch of spring rolls and cook over a moderate heat for 3–4 minutes until golden brown on all sides. Remove from the oil with a slotted spoon and drain on kitchen paper. Repeat with the remaining spring rolls.
- Remove the toothpicks before serving and serve hot, with the dipping sauce in a separate bowl and garnished with coriander leaves.

12 square spring roll wrappers
about 750 ml/1¼ pints
  groundnut oil for deep-frying
12 toothpicks
coriander leaves, to garnish

Filling:
1 tablespoon groundnut oil
2 garlic cloves, finely chopped
50 g/2 oz bean sprouts
50 g/2 oz white cabbage,
  shredded
2 fresh shiitake mushrooms,
  shredded
20 g/¾ oz celery (leaf and stalk),
  finely chopped
1 teaspoon sugar
2 teaspoons soy sauce
50 g/2 oz dried bean thread
  noodles, soaked, drained and
  cut into short lengths with
  scissors

Preparation time: 2 minutes
Cooking time: 2 minutes

toasted chilli cashews *pad med mamuang in mapan sai prik*

1 tablespoon groundnut oil
1 garlic clove, finely chopped
250 g/8 oz Roasted Cashews
   (see page 16)
¼ teaspoon crushed dried
   chillies
1 spring onion, finely chopped
2 small fresh chillies (different
   colours), finely chopped
salt, to taste

- In a wok, heat the oil and fry the garlic until golden brown. Remove and reserve.
- Add the cashews to the oil and sprinkle the crushed dried chillies over them. Stir-fry for 1 minute, then add the spring onion, chopped fresh chillies and salt to taste.
- Serve warm.

crispy rice *kao tod grob*

If you have a microwave, you can precook the patties for 3 minutes on High (100% power) before deep-frying. This will give them a slightly less chewy texture.

250 g/8 oz cold cooked rice
about 750 ml/1¼ pints
   groundnut oil for deep-frying
Plum Sauce (see page 112)

- Form the rice into about 25 small patties.
- Heat the oil for deep-frying in a wok, pop in a batch of rice patties and cook over a moderate heat for about 3 minutes or until golden. Remove from the oil with a slotted spoon and drain on kitchen paper. Repeat with the remaining patties.
- Serve hot, with the sauce in a separate bowl.

Makes about 25
Preparation time: 5 minutes
Cooking time: about 3 minutes

about 500 g/1 lb vegetables of your choice
1 large fresh red chilli, sliced lengthways, to garnish

Yellow Bean Sauce:
125 g/4 oz yellow bean sauce
½ onion, chopped
1 tablespoon tamarind water
200 ml/7 fl oz coconut milk
200 ml/7 fl oz water
2 eggs
3 tablespoons sugar
1 tablespoon soy sauce

Preparation time: 15 minutes
Cooking time: 5–6 minutes

raw vegetables with yellow bean sauce *tow jio lon*

Good vegetables to choose for this dish are peeled broccoli stalks, carrot, cucumber and courgette sticks, French beans, Chinese leaves, cauliflower florets and strips of red and yellow pepper.

- Choose a mixture of raw vegetables and chop them into bite-sized pieces.
- Make the sauce: blend the yellow bean sauce and the onion in a blender or food processor and turn into a saucepan. Add the rest of the sauce ingredients and bring gradually to the boil, stirring. Remove from the heat and pour into a bowl.
- Garnish the sauce with the sliced chilli and serve warm, with the vegetables.

2 x 250 g/8 oz blocks ready-fried tofu, sliced

200 g/7 oz fresh shiitake mushrooms

8–12 satay sticks

Marinade:

125 ml/4 fl oz dark soy sauce

50 ml/2 fl oz water

15 g/½ oz palm sugar or light muscovado sugar

2 garlic cloves, chopped

To serve:

chunks of cucumber

spring onions, finely sliced lengthways

Satay Sauce (see page 113)

Makes 8–12

Preparation time: 10 minutes, plus 1 hour marinating

Cooking time: 2–4 minutes

mushroom and tofu satay
sate het tahu

- Cut the sliced tofu into 3.5 cm/1½ inch lengths. Cut any large mushrooms in half.
- Put the marinade ingredients in a shallow bowl, add the tofu and mushrooms and stir them around to coat them on all sides. Leave to marinate for 1 hour.
- Meanwhile, soak the satay sticks in cold water for 20–30 minutes.
- Remove the satay sticks from the water one at a time and carefully thread the tofu and mushrooms on them. Cook under a hot grill for 1–2 minutes on each side.
- Serve hot, garnished with cucumber chunks and sliced spring onions, with the sauce in a separate bowl.

Preparation time: 20 minutes
Cooking time: 10 minutes

stuffed cucumber
tang kwa yatsai

125 g/4 oz fresh mango or
  pineapple flesh
2 teaspoons cornflour
¼ teaspoon crushed dried
  chillies
1 small garlic clove, chopped
1 teaspoon finely chopped
  green pepper
2 teaspoons finely chopped
  onion
2 teaspoons finely chopped
  carrot
1 teaspoon finely chopped
  small fresh red chilli
1 cucumber
a few toothpicks

- Mash the mango or pineapple with a fork and add the cornflour. Place in a saucepan with the crushed dried chillies, garlic, green pepper, onion, carrot and fresh chilli. Cook gently, stirring occasionally, for 4–5 minutes.
- Cut the ends from the cucumber and reserve. Carefully remove the seeds from the centre – you may have to cut the cucumber in half in order to achieve this. Peel the cucumber and stuff it with the fruit mixture. Put the ends back on, secure with toothpicks and steam for 10 minutes.
- Cut into slices and serve warm.

Makes 8
Preparation time: 25 minutes
Cooking time: 12–14 minutes

stuffed green peppers

prik kiaow yat sai

For this recipe it is best to use the long green peppers that you get in Greek restaurants, rather than squat bell peppers. They should be about 2 cm/¾ inch long and 2–2.5 cm/¾ –1 inch wide at their fattest part. If you like, you can prepare the stuffing and fill the peppers in advance, then coat them in batter and deep-fry them at the last minute.

8 large, mild green peppers or
   4 bell peppers
about 750 ml/1¼ pints
   groundnut oil for deep-frying
chives, to garnish

Filling:
3 baby corns, roughly chopped
3 garlic cloves, halved
4 tablespoons groundnut oil
½ large onion, finely chopped
1 tomato, diced
2 fresh shiitake mushrooms,
   finely sliced
50 g/2 oz French beans, finely
   sliced
½ teaspoon sugar
1 tablespoon soy sauce
¼ teaspoon salt
1 teaspoon ground black
   pepper
2 eggs

Batter:
3 tablespoons cornflour
50 ml/2 fl oz water
½ teaspoon salt
¼ teaspoon ground black
   pepper

- Remove the ends from the green peppers and cut out the seeds. Set the hollow peppers aside.
- Make the filling: quickly blend the corn and garlic in a blender or food processor.
- Heat 3 tablespoons of the oil in a wok or frying pan and cook the onion for 30 seconds. Add the tomato and mushrooms and cook, stirring, for 1 minute. Add the French beans and cook for 30 seconds before adding the corn and garlic mixture, the sugar, soy sauce, salt and pepper. At this point you may need to add the remaining oil. Break the eggs into the mixture and give them a good stir. Cook for 2 minutes, remove from the heat and turn the mixture on to a plate.
- Stuff the peppers with the filling, as full as you can.
- Mix the batter ingredients together thoroughly in a bowl.
- Heat the oil for deep-frying in a wok. Coat half of the peppers in the batter, pop them in the hot oil and cook them for 6–7 minutes, moving them around gently until they are golden on all sides. Remove the peppers from the oil with a slotted spoon and drain on kitchen paper. Repeat with the remaining peppers and batter.
- Arrange the cooked peppers on a plate, garnish with chives and serve immediately.

about 30 square wonton wrappers

a little egg yolk or cornflour and water paste, to seal

about 750 ml/1¼ pints groundnut oil for deep-frying

Plum Sauce (see page 112)

Filling:

3 tablespoons groundnut oil

2 garlic cloves, chopped

3 baby corns, very finely sliced

5 fresh shiitake mushrooms, finely chopped

25 g/1 oz French beans, very finely sliced

½ onion, finely chopped

1 egg

½ teaspoon sugar

1 tablespoon soy sauce

salt and pepper, to taste

Makes about 30
Preparation time: 20 minutes
Cooking time: 3–4 minutes each batch

fried wontons
giao tod

- First make the filling: heat 2 tablespoons of the oil in a wok, add the garlic and give it a stir, then add the corn, mushrooms, French beans and onion and stir-fry for 1–2 minutes. Push the vegetables to one side of the wok, pour in the remaining oil and break the egg into it. Break the yolk and stir it around, gradually mixing in the vegetables, for about 1 minute. Add the sugar, soy sauce and salt and pepper, and mix well. Remove from the heat and set the mixture aside in a bowl.
- Put a spoonful of the filling in the centre of a wonton wrapper. Fold the wrapper over to make a triangle, then seal the edges with a little egg yolk or cornflour and water paste. Repeat with the remaining wrappers and filling.
- Heat the oil for deep-frying in a wok, pop in a batch of wontons and cook over a moderate heat for 3–4 minutes until golden brown on all sides. Remove from the oil with a slotted spoon and drain on kitchen paper. Repeat the frying process with the remaining wontons.
- Serve hot, with the sauce in a separate bowl.

Makes 16
Preparation time: 20–25 minutes
Cooking time: 30 minutes

steamed stuffed wontons *Kanom jeeb*

16 round wonton wrappers
a little groundnut oil
Soy and Vinegar Dipping Sauce
  (see page 113), to serve

Filling:
125 g/4 oz onion, roughly
  chopped
3 large garlic cloves, halved
2 tablespoons sugar
1 tablespoon salt
1 teaspoon ground black
  pepper
40 g/1½ oz cornflour
50 g/2 oz carrot, finely
  chopped
2 baby corns, finely chopped
25 g/1 oz celery (leaf and
  stalk), finely chopped
1 tablespoon finely chopped
  fresh coriander

- First make the filling: in a blender or food processor, blend together the onion, garlic, sugar, salt and pepper. Place the cornflour in a bowl, add the blended mixture to it and mix well. Add the carrot and corn and mix again. Then place the mixture in a saucepan and cook over a moderate heat, stirring constantly, until it becomes thick. Remove from the heat, add the celery and coriander and stir them in well, then turn the mixture on to a plate.
- Put 1 heaped teaspoonful of the filling in the centre of a wonton wrapper, which you have placed over your thumb and index finger. As you push the filled wonton wrapper down through the circle you have formed, tighten the top, shaping the wonton but leaving the top open. Repeat with the remaining wrappers and filling.
- Put the filled wontons upright on a small plate and put the plate in a steamer.
- Drizzle a little oil over the top of the wontons, put the lid on the steamer and leave to cook for 30 minutes.
- Serve hot or warm, with the dipping sauce in a separate bowl.

Preparation time: 5 minutes
Cooking time: 2–3 minutes

thai egg strips
kai tiaow

3 eggs, beaten

1 shallot, finely sliced

green shoots of 1 spring onion, sliced

1–2 small fresh red chillies, finely chopped

1 tablespoon chopped fresh coriander leaves

1 tablespoon groundnut oil

salt and pepper, to taste

julienne of spring onion, to garnish (optional)

- Mix all the ingredients, except the oil, in a bowl.
- Heat the oil in a frying pan or wok, pour in the egg mixture and swirl it around the pan to produce a large thin omelette. Cook for 1–2 minutes until firm.
- Slide the omelette out on to a plate and roll it up as though it were a pancake. Allow to cool.
- When the omelette is cool, cut the roll crossways into 5 mm/¼ inch or 1 cm/½ inch sections, depending on how wide you want your strips to be. Serve them still rolled up or straightened out, in a heap. Garnish with strips of spring onion, if wished.

Preparation time: 20 minutes
Cooking time: 15 minutes

son-in-law eggs
kai luk kuhy

4 hard-boiled eggs
about 750 ml/1¼ pints
   groundnut oil for deep-frying
5 shallots, finely sliced
3 large garlic cloves, finely sliced
75 ml/3 fl oz tamarind water
50 ml/2 fl oz vegetarian fish
   sauce or 1 teaspoon salt
60 g/2½ oz palm sugar or light
   muscovado sugar
100 ml/3½ fl oz water

To garnish:
2 large fresh red chillies,
   deseeded and sliced
   lengthways
fresh coriander leaves

- Shell the eggs and cut them in half lengthways.
- Heat the oil for deep-frying in a wok and add the shallots and garlic. Cook gently until golden. Remove with a slotted spoon, drain on kitchen paper and set aside.
- Slide the eggs, yolk side down, into the hot oil. Cook until golden all over, then remove with a slotted spoon. Drain and set aside.
- In a saucepan, put the tamarind water, fish sauce and sugar. Stir until the sugar has melted, then add the water. Cook for 5 minutes, stirring all the time until the sauce becomes syrupy. Lower the heat.
- Arrange the eggs, yolk side up, on a plate. Sprinkle the shallots and garlic over them. Bring the sauce to a hard boil and continue boiling until it is somewhat reduced and thickened. Remove the pan from the heat and then ladle the sauce over the eggs.
- Serve hot, garnished with the red chilli slivers and coriander leaves.

475 g/15 oz can sweetcorn
   kernels
3 garlic cloves, halved
1 coriander root, sliced
1 small fresh red or green chilli,
   roughly chopped
1 spring onion, finely chopped
75 g/3 oz rice flour or plain
   flour
1 teaspoon salt
1 teaspoon ground black
   pepper
about 750 ml/1¼ pints
   groundnut oil for deep-frying

To serve:
Pickled Cucumber and Carrot
   (see page 111)
Soy and Vinegar Dipping Sauce
   (see page 113)

corn fritters
tod mun

- Drain the sweetcorn and make the sweetcorn liquid up to 50 ml/2 fl oz with water.
- Put the sweetcorn kernels in a mixing bowl and set the measured liquid aside.
- Briefly blend the garlic, coriander root and chilli in a blender or food processor.
- Add the blended mixture to the sweetcorn kernels with the spring onion, flour, measured liquid, salt and pepper. Mix thoroughly to a thick consistency.
- Heat the oil for deep-frying in a wok and drop in the mixture, 1 tablespoonful at a time. Cook in batches for 5–6 minutes until golden, remove from the oil with a slotted spoon and drain on kitchen paper. Repeat until all the fritters are done, then arrange them on a plate.
- Serve hot, with the pickle and dipping sauce in separate bowls.

Makes 8
Preparation time: 12 minutes
Cooking time: 5–6 minutes each batch

25 square spring roll wrappers
about 750 ml/1¼ pints
  groundnut oil for deep-frying
Plum Sauce (see page 112), to
  serve

Filling:
4 baby corns, roughly chopped
125 g/4 oz drained canned
  water chestnuts, chopped
½ large onion, roughly chopped
4 large garlic cloves, halved
1 egg yolk
2 heaped tablespoons
  cornflour
50 ml/½ fl oz water
20 g/¾ oz fresh coriander, finely
  chopped
salt and pepper, to taste

Makes about 25
Preparation time: 20–25 minutes
Cooking time: 3–4 minutes each batch

golden purses
kapow tong

- First make the filling: blend together the corn, water chestnuts, onion, garlic and egg yolk in a blender or food processor.
- In a saucepan, combine the cornflour and water, add the blended mixture, the coriander and salt and pepper. Cook over a low heat until thickened, stirring all the time as the mixture burns easily. Remove from the heat and allow to cool.
- Put 1 teaspoonful of the filling in the centre of a spring roll wrapper. Fold the wrapper over to make a triangle, then pleat and fold the sides over to form a little purse. Seal with a little filling. Repeat with the remaining wrappers and filling.
- Heat the oil for deep-frying in a wok, pop in a batch of spring rolls and cook over a moderate heat for 3–4 minutes until golden on all sides. Remove with a slotted spoon and drain on kitchen paper. Repeat with the remaining spring rolls.
- Serve hot, with the sauce in a separate bowl.

vegetable balls
pak chup ben tod

½ large onion, roughly chopped
4 baby corns, roughly chopped
25 g/1 oz carrot, grated
3 dried shiitake mushrooms,
  soaked, drained and sliced
25 g/1 oz dried seaweed,
  soaked and drained
1 egg
1 teaspoon black pepper
½ teaspoon salt
4 garlic cloves, halved
150 g/5 oz mashed potato
15 g/½ oz fresh coriander
5 cm/2 inch stalk of lemon
  grass, thinly sliced
50 ml/2 fl oz water
2 tablespoons cornflour
about 750 ml/1¼ pints
  groundnut oil for deep-frying
Plum Sauce (see page 112),
  to serve

- Put the vegetables and seaweed in a blender or food processor and add the egg, pepper, salt, garlic, mashed potato, coriander and lemon grass. Blend all these ingredients to a smooth paste.
- Turn the paste into a saucepan and cook over a gentle heat, turning and stirring constantly, for 3 minutes. If the mixture is too loose, mix the water and cornflour together and add a little of it. Continue to stir and cook, adding more cornflour and water if necessary. When the mixture is the right consistency, form it into walnut-size balls and chill in the refrigerator for 15 minutes.
- Heat the oil for deep-frying in a wok. Drop in a few of the vegetable balls and deep-fry for 2–3 minutes or until golden brown. Remove from the oil with a slotted spoon and drain on kitchen paper. Repeat with the remaining vegetable balls.
- Serve hot, with the dipping sauce in a separate bowl.

Preparation time: 30 minutes, plus 15–20 minutes soaking
Cooking time: about 9 minutes

Makes 8
Preparation time: 30 minutes
Cooking time: 3–4 minutes each batch

vegetable samosas *pak sa mo sa*

- First make the filling: boil the diced potato until tender, drain and set aside. Heat the oil in a small saucepan or frying pan and fry the shallot and garlic until golden. Drain and set aside. In a saucepan, gently heat the coconut milk and curry paste, stirring until smooth, then add the potato, and the shallot and garlic mixture, together with the peas, lime juice and salt. Mash roughly, remove from the heat and set aside.
- Take 2 wonton wrappers together to make a double thickness, and put a spoonful of the potato mixture in the centre. Fold the wrappers over to make a triangle, then seal the edges with a little cornflour and water paste. Repeat with the remaining wrappers and filling.
- Heat the oil for deep-frying in a wok, pop in half the samosas and cook over a moderate heat for 3–4 minutes until golden brown on all sides. Remove from the oil with a slotted spoon and drain on kitchen paper. Repeat with the remaining samosas.
- Arrange the samosas on a serving dish, sprinkle with coriander leaves and lime juice and serve at once.

16 square wonton wrappers
a little cornflour and water
  paste, to seal
about 750 ml/1¼ pints
  groundnut oil for deep-frying

Filling:

250 g/8 oz potato, diced
1 tablespoon groundnut oil
2 tablespoons finely chopped
  shallot
2 garlic cloves, finely chopped
50 ml/2 fl oz coconut milk
2 heaped teaspoons Yellow
  Curry Paste (see page 13)
75 g/3 oz peas
juice of ½ lime
½ teaspoon salt or to taste

To serve:

fresh coriander leaves
juice of 1 lime

From left: clear soup with black fungus and spring onion: and bitter melon soup (pages 40-41)

soups

Thai vegetarian soups are generally fairly
light. They are served as one dish among
several others, and are used to refresh
the palate between mouthfuls of heavier
curries and spicy salads. Thais normally
put all the food in the centre of the table
and everyone helps themselves to whatever
they want to eat, but you can, of course,
serve a soup as a first course, or give a
bowl of soup to each person at the same
time as the rest of the meal. The noodle
soups are slightly more substantial and
are often eaten as a snack, served at street
food stalls, especially for breakfast or late
at night. They are made with rice or bean
noodles, which are nourishing and easy
to digest, and less heavy than egg noodles.
Even so, I have noticed that some of the
noodles are frequently left in the bottom of
the bowl.

2 bitter melons or marrows (about 25 cm/10 inches long)

250 g/8 oz block ready-fried tofu, diced

½ onion, chopped

25 g/1 oz dried black fungus, soaked and drained, or button
mushrooms, roughly chopped

1 coriander root

2 garlic cloves, halved

2 tablespoons groundnut oil

2 eggs

2 teaspoons soy sauce

1 teaspoon ground black pepper

1 teaspoon salt

750 ml/1¼ pints Vegetable Stock (see page 19)

To serve:

fresh coriander leaves

Crispy Garlic (see page 15)

Preparation time: 10 minutes, plus 15–20 minutes soaking
Cooking time: 10 minutes

stuffed bitter melon soup
tom jieu mala yatsai

- Cut the ends from the melon and discard, then cut the melon crossways into four equal pieces. Carefully remove the seeds and pith from each piece of melon, then set the pieces aside.
- Blend together the tofu, onion, mushrooms, coriander and garlic in a blender or food processor.
- Heat the oil in a wok and add the blended mixture, 1 egg, the soy sauce, pepper and salt. Stir and mix well together for 1–2 minutes. Remove from the heat, turn into a bowl and allow to cool.
- When the mixture has cooled, add the remaining egg to bind it, then stuff the pieces of melon with it. Place the melon in a steamer and steam for 10 minutes until cooked. Meanwhile, simmer the stock.
- To serve: carefully transfer the pieces of melon to a serving bowl and ladle the hot stock over them. Garnish with coriander leaves and sprinkle with crispy garlic.

Preparation time: 10 minutes, plus 15–20 minutes soaking
Cooking time: 7 minutes

clear soup with black fungus and spring onion
tom jieu het ton hom

- Bring the stock to the boil in a saucepan. Add the rest of the ingredients, except the crispy garlic, then lower the heat to a simmer and cook for 2 minutes.
- Serve hot, garnished with the crispy garlic.

600 ml/1 pint Vegetable Stock (see page 19)

1 teaspoon sugar

½ teaspoon soy sauce

125 g/4 oz dried black fungus, soaked, drained and chopped

25 g/1 oz celery (leaf and stalk), finely chopped

25 g/1 oz spring onion, sliced lengthways

salt and pepper, to taste

1 teaspoon Crispy Garlic (see page 15), to garnish

125 g/4 oz cucumber, roughly chopped

1 onion, halved

2 garlic cloves, halved

50 g/2 oz white cabbage, chopped

600 ml/1 pint water

125 g/4 oz dried bean thread noodles, soaked and drained

25 g/1 oz dried tofu sheets, soaked, drained and torn

15 g/½ oz dried lily flowers, soaked and drained, or drained canned bamboo
 shoots, thinly sliced

1 teaspoon salt

1 teaspoon sugar

½ teaspoon soy sauce

2 large dried shiitake mushrooms, soaked, drained and thinly sliced

chopped celery leaves, to garnish

Preparation time: 10 minutes, plus 2–3 hours soaking
Cooking time: about 5 minutes

glass noodle soup
wonsen nam

- Put the cucumber, onion, garlic and cabbage in a blender or food processor and blend for 15 seconds. Turn into a saucepan and add the water. Bring to the boil, then lower the heat and cook for 2 minutes, stirring occasionally.
- Strain the stock into a larger saucepan and add the noodles, tofu, lily flowers, salt, sugar and soy sauce. Stir, then cook over a moderate heat for about 3 minutes.
- Taste to check the seasoning.
- Finally, pour the soup into a serving bowl, arrange the mushroom slices in the centre and sprinkle with chopped celery leaves.
- Serve hot.

750 ml/1¼ pints Vegetable Stock (see page 19)

3 spring onions, cut into 2.5 cm/1 inch lengths

2 baby corns, sliced obliquely

1 tomato, quartered

1 onion, cut into 8 pieces

6 lime leaves

1 celery stalk, chopped

½ x 250 g/8 oz block ready-fried tofu, diced

1 tablespoon soy sauce

1 teaspoon ground black pepper

1 heaped teaspoon crushed dried chillies

175 g/6 oz dried wide rice noodles, soaked and
   drained

To serve:

fresh coriander sprigs

lime quarters

Preparation time: 10 minutes, plus 15–20 minutes soaking

Cooking time: 8 minutes

rice noodle soup
kao tom

- Heat the stock in a saucepan and add all of the ingredients except the noodles.
- Bring to the boil for 30 seconds, then lower the heat to a simmer and cook for 5 minutes.
- Add the noodles and simmer for another 2 minutes.
- To serve: pour into a serving bowl, garnish with coriander sprigs and serve with lime quarters.

Preparation time: 5 minutes
Cooking time: 5 minutes

quick rice porridge
kao tom

200 g/7 oz cooked rice

2 small purple aubergines, roughly chopped

500 ml/17 fl oz Vegetable Stock (see page 19)

2 teaspoons soy sauce

¼ teaspoon sugar

1 cm/½ inch piece of fresh root ginger, peeled and finely sliced

1 tablespoon Crispy Garlic (see page 15)

1 tablespoon Crispy Shallots (see page 15)

salt and pepper to taste

1 spring onion, finely chopped, to garnish

This is the kind of thing Thais will eat for breakfast; it is made with rice leftover from the day before.

◉ Put the rice and aubergines in a blender or food processor together with the stock and blend until smooth.

◉ Pour the mixture into a saucepan and heat until just boiling. Add the soy sauce, sugar, ginger, garlic and shallots. Lower the heat and stir for 1 minute.

◉ Turn into a serving bowl, garnish with the chopped spring onion and serve hot.

khun tom's chilled asparagus soup
tom jieu nomai farang

300 g/10 oz asparagus

½ teaspoon salt

300 ml/½ pint water

1 tablespoon groundnut oil

1 garlic clove, finely chopped

1 shallot, sliced

½ teaspoon crushed dried chillies

½ teaspoon ground white pepper

300 ml/½ pint coconut milk

1 tablespoon vegetarian fish sauce or soy sauce

◉ Cook the asparagus in the salted water for 10–12 minutes until tender. Drain the asparagus and reserve the water. Cut the tips off the asparagus and reserve for the garnish, then purée the remaining asparagus and its liquid in a blender or food processor. Set aside.

◉ Heat the oil in a saucepan and add the garlic, shallot, chillies and pepper. Sauté for 1 minute, then add the puréed asparagus. Bring to the boil and add the coconut milk. Boil for 2 minutes, add the fish sauce and remove from the heat. Allow to cool, then cover and chill in the refrigerator for about 4 hours.

◉ Serve chilled, garnished with the reserved asparagus tips.

Preparation time: 5 minutes, plus about 4 hours chilling
Cooking time: about 20 minutes

1 teaspoon finely sliced lemon grass

1 teaspoon peeled and finely sliced galangal

1 tablespoon basil leaves

½ green pepper, chopped

3 lime leaves

100 ml/3½ fl oz water

1 tablespoon groundnut oil

2 garlic cloves, finely chopped

10 shallots, thinly sliced

1 teaspoon crushed dried chillies

1 small fresh red chilli, chopped

500 ml/17 fl oz Vegetable Stock (see page 19)

50 g/2 oz French beans, chopped

3 tablespoons vegetarian fish sauce or soy sauce

750 g/1½ lb cubed peeled pumpkin

1 teaspoon sugar

1 teaspoon ground white pepper

1 tablespoon Crushed Roasted Peanuts (see page 16)
  or crunchy peanut butter

3 teaspoons curry powder

175 ml/6 fl oz coconut milk

2 teaspoons cornflour

Crispy Basil (see page 16), to garnish

Preparation time: 30 minutes
Cooking time: 15 minutes

khun tom's pumpkin soup
tom jieu fak ton

- Blend the lemon grass, galangal, basil, green pepper, lime leaves and water in a blender or food processor, then strain and throw away the water, but reserving the purée.
- Heat the oil in a large saucepan. Add the garlic, shallots and dried and fresh chillies and stir-fry over a high heat for 1 minute.
- Add the purée, 400 ml/14 fl oz of the stock, the French beans, fish sauce and pumpkin. Stir over a moderate heat. Add the sugar, pepper, peanuts and curry powder and stir again. When the pumpkin is tender, after about 10 minutes, add the coconut milk and bring to a hard boil for 1 minute.
- Blend the remaining stock with the cornflour until smooth, add to the soup and stir to thicken.
- Ladle the soup into a large serving bowl and place the basil on top, in the centre.

1 tablespoon groundnut oil

50 g/2 oz spring onions (including green shoots), sliced

25 g/1 oz garlic, sliced

200 ml/7 fl oz coconut milk

400 ml/14 fl oz Vegetable Stock (see page 19)

¼ teaspoon ground white pepper

3 teaspoons vegetarian fish sauce or soy sauce

¼ teaspoon salt

½ teaspoon sugar

1 large banana, peeled and cut obliquely into thin slices

1 large fresh red chilli, sliced obliquely

To garnish:

fresh coriander leaves

2 limes, quartered

spring onion strips

Preparation time: 15 minutes
Cooking time: 8 minutes

banana soup
tom kuay

- Heat the oil in a saucepan and fry the sliced spring onion and garlic quite fast. Add all the other ingredients in order, and cook for 5 minutes.
- If you like, this soup can be blended: set aside about one-quarter of the banana and chilli slices, then purée the rest with the soup in a blender or food processor until smooth. Return the blended mixture to the pan, add the reserved banana and chilli slices and warm through for 3 minutes.
- Serve hot, garnished with coriander leaves, lime quarters and spring onion strips.

about 750 ml/1¼ pints groundnut oil for deep-frying

250 g/8 oz block ready-fried tofu, diced

750 ml/1¼ pints water

1 lemon grass stalk

3 lime leaves

2.5 cm/1 inch piece of galangal, peeled and sliced

1½ teaspoons salt

1 teaspoon sugar

10 small fresh green chillies

3 tablespoons lime juice

1 teaspoon vegetarian fish sauce or soy sauce

2 spring onions, sliced lengthways

1 carrot, cut into matchsticks

1 fresh shiitake mushroom, finely sliced

a handful of fresh coriander leaves, to garnish

Preparation time: 15 minutes
Cooking time: 20 minutes

tofu soup *nam tahu*

- Heat the oil for deep-frying in a wok and deep-fry the tofu dice in it until they are golden, about 3 minutes. Drain and leave on one side.
- Make a stock by boiling up the water, lemon grass, lime leaves, galangal, salt and sugar for about 10 minutes. Remove from the heat.
- Chop the green chillies and add them to the stock, together with the lime juice, fish sauce, sliced spring onions, carrot and mushroom. Cook over a moderate heat for about 6 minutes.
- Serve hot, garnished with coriander leaves.

Preparation time: 5 minutes
Cooking time: 9–10 minutes

hot sour soup with mooli radish

gang som pak gaged

750 ml/1¼ pints Vegetable
   Stock (see page 19)

1 tablespoon Red Curry Paste
   (see page 12)

1 mooli radish, peeled and
   sliced

2 teaspoons salt

40 g/1½ oz palm sugar or light
   muscovado sugar

2 tablespoons vegetarian fish
   sauce or soy sauce

3 tablespoons tamarind water

50 g/2 oz fresh spinach (leaves
   and stalks), torn

- Heat the stock in a saucepan, add the curry paste and stir until amalgamated. Bring to the boil and add the mooli. Lower the heat and add the salt, sugar, fish sauce and tamarind water. Cook for a few minutes until the mooli slices are tender.
- Put the spinach in the bottom of a serving bowl and pour the soup on top.
- Serve at once.

hot sour soup with palm hearts

tom jieu yod tan

300 ml/½ pint water

2 tablespoons soy sauce

1 teaspoon salt

½ teaspoon sugar

3 lemon grass stalks, cut into
   2.5 cm/1 inch lengths

2.5 cm/1 inch piece of galangal,
   peeled and sliced

3 lime leaves, torn

125 g/4 oz drained canned
   palm hearts, chopped

500 ml/17 fl oz coconut milk

1 tomato, cut into 8 pieces

1 tablespoon lime juice

½ teaspoon crushed dried
   chillies

- Put the water, soy sauce, salt, sugar, lemon grass, galangal and lime leaves in a saucepan. Bring to the boil and simmer for 5 minutes.
- Add the palm hearts, coconut milk, tomato, lime juice and chillies. Bring back to the boil, lower the heat and simmer for a further 5 minutes.
- Serve hot.

Preparation time: 12 minutes
Cooking time: 15 minutes

salads

Salad or 'yam' dishes appear as part of almost every Thai meal. They are sometimes made with raw fruit or vegetables, and sometimes with lightly cooked vegetables. They are usually very chilli hot, and may arrive just before the rest of the food so you have something to pick at while you finish your drink. The basic 'dressing' consists of chilli, lime or lemon juice, fish sauce or soy sauce, sugar and garlic – all very strong individual flavours that combine to make the taste of Thailand. The following recipes are all well-known combinations, but you can experiment with different variations and vegetables to discover your own favourite.

125 g/4 oz French beans, trimmed
2 garlic cloves, halved
8 small fresh green chillies, roughly chopped
2½ tablespoons vegetarian fish sauce or soy sauce
25 g/1 oz palm sugar or light muscovado sugar
4 tomatoes, chopped
50 g/2 oz Crushed Roasted Peanuts (see page 16)
juice of 2 limes
1 teaspoon salt
200 g/7 oz green papaya, peeled and grated

Preparation time: 8–9 minutes

papaya salad
som tam malago

- Cut half of the French beans into 2.5 cm/1 inch pieces. Reserve the rest whole.
- In a mortar, pound the French bean pieces, garlic and chillies until they are well broken down. Add the fish sauce, sugar, tomatoes, peanuts, lime juice and salt.
- Pound and turn all the ingredients until they are well mixed.
- Finally, add the papaya and pound again. Stir well with a large spoon to ensure everything is amalgamated.
- Turn the salad on to a serving dish and place the reserved French beans at one side.

4 hard-boiled eggs

3 shallots, finely sliced

5 small fresh green chillies, finely chopped

1 large garlic clove, finely sliced

juice of 2 limes

2 tablespoons vegetarian fish sauce or soy sauce

½ teaspoon sugar

groundnut oil for frying

25–50 g/1–2 oz basil leaves

Preparation time: 4–5 minutes
Cooking time: 1½ minutes

boiled egg salad with crispy basil

yam kai kap bai mualapa tod

- Shell the eggs and cut them in half lengthways. Put the eggs, yolk side up, on a serving dish or in a bowl and sprinkle the shallots over them. In a small bowl, put the chillies, garlic, lime juice, fish sauce and sugar and mix well together. Spoon the mixture over the eggs.
- Heat some oil in a wok, throw in the basil leaves and watch them become crispy.
- Quickly remove them from the oil with a slotted spoon and drain on kitchen paper.
- Scatter over the salad and serve.

Preparation time: 15 minutes, plus 15–20 minutes soaking
Cooking time: 3–4 minutes

glass noodle salad
yam won sen

200 g/7 oz dried glass noodles,
  soaked and drained
1 tomato, halved and sliced
20 g/¾ oz celery stalk, chopped
20 g/¾ oz spring onion,
  chopped
1 onion, halved and sliced
50 g/2 oz green pepper,
  chopped
juice of 2 limes
5 small green chillies, finely
  chopped
2 teaspoons sugar
3 tablespoons Crushed
  Roasted Peanuts (see
  page 16)
1 teaspoon crushed dried
  chillies
½ teaspoon salt
2½ tablespoons vegetarian fish
  sauce or soy sauce
fresh coriander sprigs,
  to garnish

- Cook the noodles in boiling water for 3–4 minutes, then drain and rinse them under cold water to prevent further cooking.
- Cut the noodles into 12 cm/5 inch lengths. Return them to the pan and add all the rest of the ingredients. Mix thoroughly for 2 minutes.
- Serve at room temperature, garnished with fresh coriander sprigs.

Preparation time: 8–10 minutes

cucumber salad with roasted cashews

yam tang kwa kap mamuang in mapan

1 cucumber, peeled and grated

90 g/3½ oz Roasted Cashews (see page 16)

2 teaspoons sugar

1½ teaspoons vegetarian fish sauce or soy sauce

1 teaspoon crushed dried chillies

juice of 2 limes

½ teaspoon salt

Thai cooks have an interesting method of grating vegetables and fruits. They peel cucumber by holding it flat in their left hand and chopping at it lengthways with a large knife and a quick motion, turning the cucumber round as they go. Then they scrape off what they have chopped in long strips into a bowl. Then they chop at it again and scrape it again until they reach the seeds, which they throw away.

⊙ Put all the ingredients in a bowl and mix thoroughly.

salty egg salad
yam kai kem

4 Salted Eggs (see page 110),
  shelled and sliced

25 g/1 oz fresh root ginger,
  peeled and cut into julienne

50 g/2 oz shallots, sliced

1 tablespoon finely chopped
  small red and green chillies

2 tablespoons lemon juice

1 tablespoon soy sauce

1 teaspoon sugar

a few fresh coriander sprigs, to
  garnish

- Put all the ingredients, except the coriander, in a large bowl. Mix everything together thoroughly.
- Turn the salad out on to a serving dish and garnish with coriander.

fried egg salad
yam kai tod

1 tablespoon groundnut oil

4 eggs

2 shallots, finely sliced

5 small fresh red chillies, finely
  sliced

2 garlic cloves, finely sliced

juice of 2 limes

2 tablespoons vegetarian fish
  sauce or soy sauce

1 teaspoon sugar

1 teaspoon peeled and grated
  fresh root ginger

fresh coriander sprigs, to
  garnish

- Heat the oil in a wok and crack in the eggs. Break the yolks and fry until almost firm. Remove and set aside to cool.
- In a mixing bowl, combine the rest of the ingredients thoroughly.
- Cut the fried eggs into slices and place on a serving dish. Spoon the shallot and chilli mixture over them, garnish with coriander sprigs and serve.

Preparation time: 10 minutes
Cooking time: 6 minutes

Preparation time: 12 minutes

green mango salad *yam mamuang*

- Stir the mango and shallot together in a large bowl. Add the sugar, lime juice, soy sauce, salt and chillies and stir thoroughly for 1–2 minutes.
- Add the peanuts, give the salad a final stir and turn out on to a serving dish.
- Garnish with coriander leaves before serving.

1 large, hard green mango, peeled and grated

1 shallot, chopped

30 g/1¼ oz palm sugar or light muscovado sugar

1 tablespoon lime juice

1 tablespoon soy sauce

½ teaspoon salt

1 teaspoon crushed dried chillies

50 g/2 oz Crushed Roasted Peanuts (see page 16)

fresh coriander leaves, to garnish

segments of ½ pomelo or 1 grapefruit, membranes removed and segments then halved

4 shallots, sliced

½ teaspoon crushed dried chillies

2 tablespoons sugar

2 tablespoons vegetarian fish sauce or soy sauce

juice of 2 limes

¼ teaspoon salt

Preparation time: 8 minutes

pomelo salad

yam sommo

○ For this very easy salad, simply put all the ingredients in a bowl and mix thoroughly.

50 g/2 oz runner beans or French beans, thinly sliced

100 g/3½ oz soft tofu

100 ml/3½ fl oz coconut milk

1 shallot, sliced

25 g/1 oz Crushed Roasted Peanuts (see page 16)

1 teaspoon crushed dried chillies

1 tablespoon lime juice

1 teaspoon sugar

2 tablespoons soy sauce

1 teaspoon salt

Preparation time: 10 minutes
Cooking time: 5–6 minutes

green bean salad
yam tua fak yiaow

- Boil the beans in water for 2 minutes, drain and set aside.
- Soften the tofu in the coconut milk over a gentle heat, until partly melted. Remove from the heat and add the beans and the rest of the ingredients. Stir thoroughly and turn out on to a serving dish.
- Serve at room temperature.

250 g/8 oz mooli radish, peeled
125 ml/4 fl oz groundnut oil
6 shallots, sliced
25 g/1 oz fresh mint leaves, chopped
1 teaspoon crushed dried chillies
1 tablespoon vegetarian fish sauce or soy sauce
juice of 1 lime
2 tablespoons Ground Roast Rice (see page 16)
1 egg white
fresh mint leaves, to garnish

Preparation time: 15 minutes
Cooking time: 8 minutes

mooli salad
yam maupakajin

- Cook the mooli radish in boiling water for 15 minutes. Drain, then grate, shred or mash the flesh.
- Heat the oil in a wok. While it is heating, mix the mooli radish with all the other ingredients and form into 4 patties.
- When the oil is hot, slide the patties into the wok carefully, one at a time, and cook for 2–3 minutes on each side. Remove from the oil with a slotted spoon and drain on kitchen paper.
- Serve hot, garnished with mint leaves.

Preparation time: 5 minutes, plus 15–20 minutes soaking
Cooking time: 5–6 minutes

mushroom salad
yam het

● Boil the mushrooms for 5–6 minutes, drain and place in a serving dish. Add all the rest of the ingredients and mix thoroughly.

125 g/4 oz dried black fungus, soaked and drained
15 g/½ oz celery stalk, finely sliced
1 shallot, sliced
5 small fresh green and red chillies, finely sliced
juice of 2 limes
2 teaspoons sugar
1 teaspoon salt

From top left: stir-fried mixed vegetables with cashew nuts (page 71); and Sweet and Sour Vegetables (page 71)

These dishes are all fairly substantial, but they are usually accompanied by one or two other dishes as well as rice. Thai curries can be as hot as Indian curries, if not hotter, but for the most part they taste completely different. This is because the spices used are not the same, and the tangy flavours of lime juice, lime leaves and lemon grass shine through. Thai curries are lighter and have more liquid than Indian curries, and can be made quite quickly. Stir-fries should be cooked and served at the last minute, so the vegetables retain a slightly crunchy texture.

main
dishes

Preparation time: 10 minutes
Cooking time: 5 minutes

sweet and sour vegetables
pad pak peow wan

2 tablespoons groundnut oil

3 garlic cloves, chopped

1 cucumber, halved, deseeded
and chopped obliquely into
5 mm/¼ inch slices

4 baby corns, sliced obliquely

1 tomato, cut into 8 pieces

250 g/8 oz can water
chestnuts, drained

50 g/2 oz mangetout, topped
and tailed

1 onion, roughly chopped

4 tablespoons Vegetable Stock
(see page 19)

1 tablespoon sugar

1 tablespoon vegetarian fish
sauce or soy sauce

1 tablespoon distilled
white vinegar or Chinese
rice vinegar

3 spring onions, roughly
chopped

- Heat the oil in a wok, add the garlic and fry quickly. When the garlic is turning golden, add the rest of the ingredients, except the spring onions. Cook, stirring constantly, for 2–3 minutes. Check the seasoning, then add the chopped spring onions and cook for 30 seconds.
- Serve at once.

Preparation time: 20 minutes
Cooking time: 2–3 minutes

stir-fried mixed vegetables with cashew nuts

pad pak rom mit med ma muang

- Mix all the ingredients, except the oil, in a bowl.
- Heat a wok and add the oil. Throw in the contents of the bowl and cook over a high heat, stirring and turning, for 2–3 minutes.
- Serve at once.

250 g/8 oz Chinese leaves, chopped into 2.5 cm/1 inch pieces
50 g/2 oz cauliflower florets
50 g/2 oz broccoli (preferably Chinese)
50 g/2 oz white cabbage, chopped
2 baby corns, sliced obliquely
1 tomato, cut into 8 pieces
5 garlic cloves, chopped
50 g/2 oz Roasted Cashews (see page 16)
1½ tablespoons soy sauce
1 teaspoon sugar
100 ml/3½ fl oz water
2½ tablespoons groundnut oil
ground black pepper, to taste

1 tablespoon groundnut oil

2 large garlic cloves, chopped

125 g/4 oz baby corn, sliced obliquely

10 dried shiitake mushrooms, soaked, drained
and sliced

125 g/4 oz drained canned bamboo shoots

50 g/2 oz mangetouts, topped and tailed

1 teaspoon sugar

3 tablespoons soy sauce

1 tablespoon water

ground black pepper, to taste

Preparation time: 10 minutes, plus 15–20 minutes soaking
Cooking time: 3–4 minutes

shiitake mushroom, bamboo shoot and mangetout stir-fry

pad het, nomai, tualangdao

- Heat the oil in a wok and add the garlic. Give it a quick stir around, then add all the rest of the ingredients in turn. Stir-fry over a high heat for 2–3 minutes, then turn out on to a serving dish.
- Serve at once.

1 tablespoon groundnut oil

3 eggs, beaten

salt and pepper, to taste

Crispy Basil (see pg16), to garnish

Filling:

3 tablespoons groundnut oil

2 garlic cloves, chopped

1 onion, finely chopped

2 tablespoons chopped French beans

2 tablespoons chopped asparagus

3 baby corns, thinly sliced

1 tomato, diced

4 dried shiitake mushrooms, soaked, drained and sliced

1½ teaspoons sugar

2 teaspoons soy sauce

50 ml/2 fl oz water

pinch of salt

Preparation time: 8–10 minutes, plus 15–20 minutes soaking

Cooking time: 8–10 minutes

stuffed omelette
kai yat sai

- First make the filling: heat the 3 tablespoons oil in a wok, add the garlic and onion and stir-fry for 30 seconds. Add the beans, asparagus, corn, tomato, mushrooms, sugar and soy sauce and stir-fry for 3–4 minutes, then add the water and salt and continue stir-frying for 2 minutes. Remove the filling from the wok and set aside.
- Wipe the wok clean with kitchen paper.
- Make the omelette: put the 1 tablespoon oil in the wok and heat it, making sure the oil coats not only the base of the wok but as much of the sides as possible. Pour off any excess. Pour in the beaten eggs, swirling them around in the wok to form a large, thin omelette. Loosen the omelette and move it around with a spatula to make sure it is not sticking to the wok, adding a touch more oil if necessary.
- When the omelette is almost firm, put the filling in the middle and fold both sides and ends over to form an oblong parcel, constantly ensuring that the omelette is not sticking underneath.
- Carefully remove the omelette from the wok and place in a serving dish. Serve the cooked dish at once garnished with Crispy Basil.

Preparation time: 7 minutes
Cooking time: 18 minutes

eggs paolo
kai paolo

3 tablespoons groundnut oil
250 g/8 oz block ready-fried tofu, cut into 12 pieces
750 ml/1¼ pints Vegetable Stock (see page 19)
6 coriander roots
1 teaspoon ground black pepper
4 garlic cloves, halved
1 teaspoon five-spice powder
1 tablespoon dark soy sauce
4 hard-boiled eggs, shelled
100 g/3½ oz palm sugar or light muscovado sugar
1 teaspoon salt
2 teaspoons soy sauce
fresh coriander leaves, to garnish

- Heat 2 tablespoons of the oil in a wok and fry the tofu until golden. Drain and place in a saucepan with the stock. Bring to the boil, then lower the heat and simmer for 10 minutes.
- Pound the coriander roots with the pepper in a mortar, add the garlic and five-spice powder and pound again until everything is well broken down and mixed together.
- Put the dark soy sauce in a bowl and turn the eggs in it to give them colour.
- Fry the coriander root mixture in the remaining oil in the wok, then add the sugar, salt and soy sauce. Remove the tofu from the stock with a slotted spoon and add it to the wok. Add 4 tablespoons of the stock, stir well for 30 seconds, then turn the contents of the wok into the remaining stock in the saucepan and add the eggs.
- Bring to a low boil and cook for 5 minutes.
- Turn into a serving bowl, garnish with coriander leaves and serve.

vermicelli noodles with gravy
ka nom chi nam ya

500 g/1 lb dried rice vermicelli
125 g/4 oz ready-fried tofu, sliced
1 tablespoon Red Curry Paste (see page 12)
50 g/2 oz krachai or galangal, peeled and chopped
250 ml/8 fl oz coconut milk
1½ teaspoons salt
300 ml/½ pint hot water
2 teaspoons sugar
fresh coriander leaves, to garnish

- Soak the vermicelli in a bowl of warm water for 15–20 minutes.
- Meanwhile, put the tofu, curry paste, krachai, coconut milk and salt in a blender or food processor and blend until smooth. Add the hot water and blend again for 5 seconds. Pour the blended mixture into a saucepan and bring to the boil, stirring continuously. Lower the heat to a simmer and add the sugar. Continue cooking gently for 3–4 minutes.
- Drain the vermicelli and place in a serving bowl. Pour the gravy over it and sprinkle with coriander leaves.

Preparation time: 15–20 minutes
Cooking time: 9–10 minutes

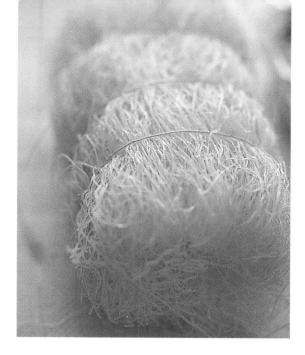

Preparation time: 6 minutes
Cooking time: 3–4 minutes

stir-fried palm hearts *pad pak yad maprow*

- Heat the oil in a wok and stir-fry the garlic for a few seconds until it is turning golden. Add all the other ingredients and stir-fry over a high heat for 2–3 minutes.
- Serve at once.

2 tablespoons groundnut oil

3 garlic cloves, sliced

2 x 425 g/14 oz cans palm hearts, drained and sliced if necessary

2 broccoli stalks, peeled and sliced, or 8 asparagus tips, blanched

50 ml/2 fl oz water

3 teaspoons sugar

¼ teaspoon salt

1 tablespoon soy sauce

ground black pepper, to taste

250 g/8 oz plain white flour

½ teaspoon salt

125 g/4 oz hard vegetable fat

2 tablespoons cold water

about 750 ml/1¼ pints groundnut oil for
 deep-frying

Hot Sweet Sauce (see page 112), to serve

Filling:

500 g/1 lb pumpkin, peeled and cut into chunks

250 ml/8 fl oz coconut milk

1 tablespoon vegetarian fish sauce or soy sauce

1 lemon grass stalk, thinly sliced

1 lime leaf, torn

1 teaspoon crushed dried chillies

1 teaspoon Red Curry Paste (see page 12)

½ red pepper, diced

½ onion, finely chopped

3 tablespoons finely diced cooked carrot

3 tablespoons finely diced canned water
 chestnuts

Makes 16

Preparation time: about 40 minutes, plus 10–15 minutes chilling

Cooking time: 10–12 minutes

thai fried pies
pie Thai tod

- First make the filling: put the pumpkin, coconut milk, fish sauce, lemon grass, lime leaf and chillies in a saucepan, bring to the boil and simmer for about 15 minutes until the pumpkin is tender. Mash the mixture in the pan and then continue to simmer if you think it is too thin: it should be fairly thick. Remove from the heat and allow to cool.
- Meanwhile, make the pastry: sift the flour and salt into a bowl. Cut the fat into small pieces and add them to the flour a little at a time, rubbing them in with your fingers until the mixture is like fine crumbs. Add the water and stir with a knife until it is incorporated. Knead the mixture quickly until a dough is formed, then chill in the refrigerator for 10–15 minutes.
- Add the remaining filling ingredients to the cold cooked filling and mix together.
- Roll out the chilled dough thinly, and cut it into sixteen 7 cm/3 inch circles.
- Divide the filling equally among the pastry circles, fold and seal with a fork.
- Heat the oil for deep-frying in a wok, pop in half of the pies and cook over a moderate heat for 5–6 minutes until golden. Remove with a slotted spoon and drain on kitchen paper. Repeat with the remaining pies.
- Serve hot or warm, with the sauce in a separate bowl.

600 ml/1 pint water

1 tablespoon Red Curry Paste (see page 12)

20 fresh lychees, stoned, or 500 g/1 lb can lychees, drained and juice reserved

1¼ teaspoons salt

4 small round aubergines, quartered

50 g/2 oz green beans, chopped into 2.5 cm/1 inch lengths

6 lime leaves, torn

20 g/¾ oz krachai or galangal, unpeeled

4 baby corns

15 g/½ oz green peppercorns

2 large fresh green chillies

2 teaspoons sugar

20 g/¾ oz cucumber, diced

Preparation time: 7–10 minutes
Cooking time: 8 minutes

forest curry with lychees *gang pa linji*

- Heat the water in a saucepan, add the curry paste and stir to blend thoroughly. If you are using canned lychees, add the reserved juice now, then add the salt and bring to the boil, stirring.
- Lower the heat to a slow boil and add all the other ingredients except the lychees and cucumber. Stir for 30 seconds.
- Add the lychees and cucumber and cook, stirring occasionally, for 3–4 minutes.

Preparation time: 3 minutes
Cooking time: 7–9 minutes

dry banana curry
panang gluay

In Thailand there are 28 varieties of gluay, the generic term for banana or plantain. If you prefer to use plantain for this recipe you will need the smallish, orangey-pink-skinned kind, not the large green-skinned ones. Unripe bananas are easier to find.

- Bring the coconut milk and curry paste to the boil in a saucepan or wok and simmer, stirring, for 3–4 minutes. Add the banana and 3 of the lime leaves and cook for 4–5 minutes. Garnish with the remaining lime leaves, cut into thin strips.

300 ml/½ pint coconut milk
1 heaped tablespoon Panang Curry Paste (see page 14)
4 unripe bananas, peeled and quartered
5 lime leaves

Preparation time: 5 minutes, plus 15–20 minutes soaking
Cooking time: 7–10 minutes

steamed broccoli with mushrooms
kanah gab het ning

200 g/7 oz broccoli (florets and
  stalks)
10 dried shiitake mushrooms,
  soaked, drained and cut into
  thirds
2 tablespoons vegetarian fish
  sauce or soy sauce
½ teaspoon salt
½ teaspoon sugar

To serve:
soy sauce
sesame oil
sugar

- Separate the broccoli florets and stalks. Peel the stalks and, if they are thick, cut them into thin slices lengthways.
- Put the vegetables on a plate and sprinkle them with the fish sauce, salt and sugar.
- Put the plate in a steamer and steam until cooked, about 7–10 minutes. Carefully remove the plate from the steamer.
- To serve: mix a little soy sauce with a little sesame oil and sugar, heat it up in a small saucepan, then drizzle it over the steamed vegetables.

Preparation time: 7 minutes
Cooking time: 10 minutes

green curry with straw mushrooms

gangkio won gabhet

300 ml/½ pint coconut milk

40 g/1½ oz Green Curry Paste
(see page 12)

300 ml/½ pint Vegetable Stock
(see page 19)

4 small round aubergines, each
cut into 8 pieces

40 g/1½ oz palm sugar or light
muscovado sugar

1 teaspoon salt

4 teaspoons vegetarian fish
sauce or soy sauce

25 g/1 oz krachai or galangal,
peeled

425 g/14 oz can straw
mushrooms, drained

50 g/2 oz green pepper, thinly
sliced

To garnish:

a handful of fresh basil leaves

2 tablespoons coconut milk

- Heat the coconut milk in a saucepan with the curry paste. Stir to amalgamate. Add the stock and then the aubergines, sugar, salt, fish sauce, krachai and mushrooms.
- Bring to the boil and cook, stirring, for 2 minutes. Add the green pepper, lower the heat and cook for 1 minute.
- Serve in a bowl, garnished with the basil leaves and drizzled coconut milk.

150 ml/¼ pint Vegetable Stock (see page 19)

8 lime leaves

25 g/1 oz galangal, peeled and sliced

175 g/6 oz carrots, cut into chunks

4 garlic cloves, crushed

2 large fresh chillies (red and green)

1 tablespoon groundnut oil

2 tablespoons Crushed Roasted Peanuts (see page 16)

300 ml/½ pint coconut milk

2 tablespoons Yellow Curry Paste (see page 13)

8 canned straw mushrooms, drained

4 shallots

½ teaspoon salt or to taste

Preparation time: 15 minutes
Cooking time: 35–40 minutes

yellow curry with carrot
gang gallee gup carrot

- Put the stock in a saucepan, add 5 of the lime leaves, the galangal, carrots, half of the crushed garlic and the whole chillies. Simmer for 15 minutes.
- Strain the stock, reserving the liquid and both the carrots and chillies separately.
- Heat the oil in a saucepan and fry the remaining garlic for 1 minute. Add the reserved carrot and the peanuts and cook, stirring, for 1 minute. Add the coconut milk and curry paste and stir until well blended. Now add the reserved liquid, the whole mushrooms and shallots and simmer, stirring occasionally, for 15 minutes or until the shallots are cooked. Add salt.
- Deseed and finely slice the reserved cooked chillies. Use as a garnish for the curry, together with the remaining lime leaves.

Preparation time: 10 minutes
Cooking time: 15 minutes

pineapple red curry

gaeng pet sapparote

100 ml/3½ fl oz coconut milk
1 tablespoon Red Curry Paste
  (see page 12)
500 g/1 lb chopped fresh
  pineapple
450 ml/¾ pint water
25 g/1 oz palm sugar or light
  muscovado sugar
1½ teaspoons salt
1 tablespoon lime juice
1 tablespoon soy sauce

○ Mix the coconut milk and curry paste together in a saucepan over a low heat. Add the rest of the ingredients and bring slowly to the boil, stirring occasionally. Lower the heat and simmer for 10 minutes.

400 g/13 oz potato

750 ml/1¼ pints coconut milk

2 tablespoons Massaman Curry Paste (see page 14) or, to taste

50 g/2 oz Crushed Roasted Peanuts (see page 16)

1 large onion, chopped

75 ml/3 fl oz tamarind water

75 g/3 oz palm sugar or light muscovado sugar

2 teaspoons salt

fresh basil leaves, to garnish

Preparation time: 8 minutes
Cooking time: 20–25 minutes

massaman potato curry *gang massaman*

- Chop the potato into equal-size chunks. Heat the coconut milk in a saucepan and add the curry paste. Stir to amalgamate, then bring to a simmer. Lower the heat, add the potato and cook for 6 minutes.
- Add the peanuts, onion, tamarind water, sugar and salt. Stir well to dissolve the sugar and continue to simmer, stirring, for 5 minutes.
- Raise the heat and let the liquid bubble until the potato is tender.
- Garnish with basil leaves before serving.

rice and *noodles*

Fried rice dishes are a wonderful way of using up rice that was not eaten on a previous occasion because they are best made with rice that has been cooked and allowed to cool. If the rice has only just been cooked and is still warm, it absorbs too much instead of just being coated. I always freeze leftover rice for just this purpose. If you need to produce a meal in a hurry or unexpectedly, you can usually find an onion, a few vegetables and possibly an egg or two, which you can quickly turn into a delicious and beautiful-looking meal. There are many different kinds of noodles, most of which just require soaking in a bowl of warm water for 15–20 minutes before use, or you can deep-fry them straight from the packet.

Preparation time: 15 minutes, plus 15–20 minutes soaking
Cooking time: 8 minutes

thai fried noodles
pad thai

3 tablespoons groundnut oil
175 g/6 oz ready-fried tofu, diced
1 tablespoon chopped garlic
125 g/4 oz bean thread noodles, soaked and drained
25 g/1 oz carrot, grated
2 tablespoons distilled white vinegar or Chinese rice vinegar
2 tablespoons soy sauce
100 ml/3½ fl oz water
2 eggs
3 teaspoons sugar
2 spring onions, sliced
¼ teaspoon ground black pepper

To serve:
1 tablespoon Crushed Roasted Peanuts (see page 16)
125 g/4 oz bean sprouts
1 spring onion, sliced in half lengthways

- Heat a wok and add 2 tablespoons of the oil. When the oil is hot, add the tofu and fry, stirring, until golden brown on all sides.
- Add the garlic, noodles, carrot, vinegar, soy sauce and water, stirring continuously.
- Push the contents of the wok to one side, leaving a space into which to break the eggs. Break the yolks and stir around, gradually incorporating the noodle mixture.
- Pour the remaining oil into the wok and add the rest of the ingredients. Cook for 2–3 minutes, stirring and shaking the wok all the time.
- To serve: heap the noodle mixture on to a plate, then sprinkle with the peanuts. Serve with the bean sprouts and spring onion halves.

fried rice with palm hearts
kao pad yod kaprow on

1 tablespoon groundnut oil
3 garlic cloves, chopped
¼ red pepper, chopped
125 g/4 oz drained canned palm hearts, chopped
125 g/4 oz drained canned straw mushrooms
250 g/8 oz cold cooked rice
½ teaspoon sugar
1 tablespoon soy sauce
¼ teaspoon salt
¼ teaspoon ground black pepper
fresh coriander leaves, to garnish

- Heat the oil in a wok over a moderate heat, then add the rest of the ingredients in order, giving a quick stir to each. When all the ingredients are in the wok, stir the rice around to break it up and mix it in.
- Increase the heat to high and stir-fry for 3–4 minutes, making sure the mixture is not sticking.
- Turn into a bowl, garnish with coriander leaves and serve.

Preparation time: 4 minutes
Cooking time: 5–6 minutes

Preparation time: 4 minutes
Cooking time: 20 minutes

steamed rice with fried eggs
kao pad kai

250 g/8 oz rice

2 tablespoons groundnut oil

1 shallot, finely chopped

2 garlic cloves, finely chopped

1 fresh red chilli, chopped

50 g/2 oz button mushrooms, chopped

25 g/1 oz fresh basil leaves

4 eggs

- Wash and steam the rice (see page 18).
- While the rice is cooking, heat 1 tablespoon of the oil in a wok or frying pan and add the shallot, garlic and chilli. Stir-fry for 30 seconds and then add the mushrooms. Stir-fry for 2 minutes and then add the basil. Increase the heat to high and cook, stirring, for 30 seconds. Remove from the wok and set aside.
- When the rice is cooked, pour the remaining oil into a frying pan and fry the eggs.
- Put a serving of rice on each plate and top with a fried egg. Arrange a serving of the mushroom and basil mixture on the side.

steamed rice with chilli
kao gab prik

375 g/12 oz rice

1 tablespoon groundnut oil

4 garlic cloves, chopped

4 large fresh red chillies, sliced

50 g/2 oz drained canned straw mushrooms

50 g/2 oz oyster mushrooms, torn

125 g/4 oz drained canned bamboo shoots

1 teaspoon sugar

½ teaspoon salt

1 teaspoon soy sauce

fresh coriander sprigs, to garnish

- Cook the rice in the normal way (see page 18).
- While the rice is cooking, heat the oil in a wok and add the garlic and chillies. Stir-fry for 30 seconds before adding the mushrooms and bamboo shoots. Stir-fry again for 1 minute, then lower the heat and add the sugar, salt and soy sauce. Give the mixture another good stir, then taste and adjust the seasoning.
- Serve the vegetables over the steamed rice, garnished with coriander.

Preparation time: 8 minutes
Cooking time: 20 minutes

curried rice with black fungus
kao gearg pet het hoo noo

2 tablespoons groundnut oil
1 onion, chopped
125 g/4 oz dried black fungus, soaked, drained and sliced
250 g/8 oz cold cooked rice
1 teaspoon curry powder
½ teaspoon soy sauce
2 tomatoes, chopped small
salt and pepper, to taste
1 tablespoon Crispy Garlic (see page 16), to garnish

- Heat the oil in a wok over a moderate heat, then add all of the ingredients in order, making sure the rice is well mixed in.
- Increase the heat to high and stir-fry for 3–4 minutes.
- Turn into a bowl, garnish with the crispy garlic and serve.

Preparation time: 10 minutes, plus 15–20 minutes soaking
Cooking time: 5 minutes

coconut rice with battered vegetables
kao maprow gab

250 g/8 oz rice
475 ml/16 fl oz coconut milk
125 g/4 oz mushrooms
125 g/4 oz courgettes, cut into 5 mm/¼ inch slices
125 g/4 oz aubergine, cut into 5 mm/¼ inch slices
groundnut oil for deep-frying

Batter:
75 g/3 oz rice or plain flour
175 ml/6 fl oz water
1 teaspoon Green Curry Paste (see page 12)

To serve:
bottled chilli sauce
Soy and Vinegar Dipping Sauce

- Cook the rice in the normal way (see page 8), but use the coconut milk instead of water to boil it in. When draining the rice for steaming, reserve the coconut milk and use it again, mixed with water, as the steaming liquid.
- While the rice is cooking, make a light batter with the flour, water and curry paste.
- Heat the oil for deep-frying in a wok. Coat all the vegetables in the batter and deep-fry in batches over a moderate heat for 3–4 minutes until golden. Remove from the oil with a slotted spoon and drain on kitchen paper.
- To serve: put the rice in the centre of a dish and arrange the deep-fried vegetables around it. Serve hot, with some chilli sauce and Soy and Vinegar Dipping Sauce (see page 113), in separate bowls.

Preparation time: 15 minutes
Cooking time: 30 minutes

2 tablespoons groundnut oil

500 g/1 lb cold cooked rice

125 g/4 oz mangetouts, topped
and tailed

125 g/4 oz button mushrooms,
halved

125 g/4 oz drained canned
bamboo shoots

1 teaspoon turmeric powder

2 teaspoons sugar

1 tablespoon soy sauce

1 teaspoon salt

ground black pepper, to taste

To garnish:

1 tablespoon Crispy Garlic
(see page 15)

1 large fresh red chilli,
deseeded and cut into strips

Preparation time: 3 minutes
Cooking time: 3–4 minutes

yellow rice with mushrooms
kao leung gab het

○ Heat the oil in a wok. Add the rice and give it a good stir, then add the rest of the ingredients. Stir-fry over a low heat until thoroughly mixed. Increase the heat and stir and turn for 1–2 minutes, making sure the rice does not stick to the wok.

○ Turn on to a serving dish, garnish with the garlic and chilli and serve at once.

1 pineapple

2 tablespoons groundnut oil

1 tablespoon Yellow Curry
Paste (see page 13)

50 g/2 oz Crushed Roasted
Peanuts (see page 16)

50 g/2 oz dried black fungus,
soaked, drained and chopped

4 shallots, finely sliced

2 tablespoons sugar

1½ teaspoons salt

juice of ½ lime

2 teaspoons soy sauce

2 eggs

500 g/1 lb cold cooked rice

To serve:

1 large fresh red chilli,
deseeded and chopped
obliquely

fresh coriander sprigs

pineapple fried rice
kao pad sapporote

○ Halve the pineapple lengthways, carefully scoop out all the flesh and then chop it into small chunks.

○ Reserve both the shells and the chopped flesh.

○ Heat the oil in a wok and add the curry paste. Cook over a gentle heat for 1 minute, then add the pineapple, peanuts, mushrooms, shallots, sugar, salt, lime juice and soy sauce. Stir-fry over a moderate heat for 1–2 minutes.

○ Push the contents of the wok to one side and crack 2 eggs into the middle. Stir them around and gradually incorporate the other ingredients. Add the rice and stir-fry vigorously for 2–3 minutes over a high heat.

○ To serve: carefully spoon the mixture into the pineapple shells, garnish with the chilli and coriander and serve at once.

Preparation time: 25 minutes, plus 15–20 minutes soaking
Cooking time: 10 minutes

Preparation time: 10 minutes
Cooking time: 6 minutes

fried rice with beans and tofu
kao pad tahu

about 750 ml/1¼ pints groundnut oil for deep-frying

½ × 250 g/8 oz block ready-fried tofu, diced

2 eggs

250 g/8 oz cold cooked rice

3 teaspoons sugar

1½ tablespoons soy sauce

2 teaspoons crushed dried chillies

1 teaspoon vegetarian fish sauce or salt

125 g/4 oz French beans, finely chopped

25 g/1 oz Crispy Mint (see page 16), to serve

- Heat the oil for deep-frying in a wok and deep-fry the tofu over a moderate heat until golden brown on all sides. Remove from the oil with a slotted spoon, drain on kitchen paper and set aside.
- Pour the oil out of the wok, leaving behind about 2 tablespoonfuls. Heat this oil until hot, then crack the eggs into it, breaking the yolks and stirring them around.
- Add the rice, sugar, soy sauce, chillies and fish sauce and increase the heat to high.
- Stir-fry vigorously for 1 minute.
- Lower the heat and add the French beans and tofu. Increase the heat again and stir-fry vigorously for 1 minute.
- Turn on to a dish and serve with the crispy mint.

2–3 tablespoons groundnut oil

4 baby corns, sliced

1 tomato, diced

1 onion, sliced

1 celery stalk and leaf, finely chopped

50 g/2 oz French beans, finely chopped

2 eggs

425 g/14 oz cold cooked rice

2 teaspoons sugar

3 tablespoons soy sauce

salt and pepper, to taste

fresh coriander sprigs, to garnish

fried rice
kao pad

- Heat the oil in a wok over a fairly high heat. Throw in the vegetables and give them all a good vigorous stir. Break the eggs into the vegetables and stir around well. Add the rice and stir-fry over a high heat for 30 seconds, mixing well. Lower the heat and add the sugar, soy sauce, salt and pepper. Increase the heat once more for a final stir and turn.
- Serve at once, garnished with coriander sprigs.

Preparation time: 7–8 minutes
Cooking time: 5 minutes

chiang mai noodles
kow soi

175 g/6 oz dried egg noodles

1 tablespoon groundnut oil

2 garlic cloves, finely chopped

2 tablespoons Red Curry Paste (see page 12)

¼ teaspoon crushed dried chillies

250 ml/8 fl oz coconut milk

500 ml/17 fl oz Vegetable Stock (see page 19)

¼ teaspoon turmeric powder

1½ teaspoons curry powder

2 tablespoons vegetarian fish sauce or soy sauce

15 g/½ oz palm sugar or light muscovado sugar

25 g/1 oz celery stalk, chopped

25 g/1 oz shallot, finely sliced

25 g/1 oz red pepper, chopped

25 g/1 oz dried shiitake mushrooms, soaked, drained and sliced

1 tablespoon Crushed Roasted Peanuts (see page 16)

To serve:

2 tablespoons lime juice

25 g/1 oz each pickled cabbage and shallot

The pickled cabbage and shallot served with this dish are taken from the Rice Water Pickle (see page 110).

- Cook the noodles in boiling water for 5–6 minutes. Drain and rinse in cold water to stop further cooking.
- Heat the oil in a wok, add the garlic and stir-fry until golden. Add the curry paste and chillies and mix thoroughly. Pour in the coconut milk, stirring continuously, then bring to the boil and cook until the liquid thickens a little.
- Add the stock, turmeric and curry powders, fish sauce and sugar and bring back to the boil. Lower the heat and add the celery, shallot, red pepper, mushrooms and peanuts. Bring back to the boil and then remove from the heat.
- To serve: put the noodles in a large serving bowl and pour the sauce over them.
- Sprinkle with lime juice to taste and serve with the pickled cabbage and shallot.

Preparation time: 30 minutes, plus 15–20 minutes soaking
Cooking time: 15 minutes

stir-fried rice with long beans *kao pad tua fat yao*

2 tablespoons groundnut oil

150 g/5 oz courgettes, cut into 1 cm/½ inch pieces

125 g/4 oz yardlong beans or green beans, finely chopped

250 g/8 oz cold cooked rice

2 teaspoons sugar

1 teaspoon salt

2 teaspoons soy sauce

1 tablespoon Crispy Garlic (see page 15), to garnish

- Heat the oil in a wok over a moderate heat, then add all of the ingredients one by one, giving a quick stir as each one goes in.
- Increase the heat to high and stir-fry for 2–3 minutes.
- To serve: turn the rice and vegetable mixture on to a plate and garnish with the crispy garlic. Chopped spring onion, strips of red pepper and chilli can also be used as a garnish.

Preparation time: 5 minutes
Cooking time: 4 minutes

Preparation time: 5 minutes
Cooking time: 10–12 minutes

200 g/7 oz dried egg noodles

2 tablespoons groundnut oil

3 garlic cloves, chopped

1 teaspoon sugar

1 tablespoon soy sauce

1 tablespoon vegetarian fish
sauce

½ teaspoon salt

50 g/2 oz oyster mushrooms,
torn

½ onion, chopped

125 g/4 oz mangetouts, topped
and tailed

4 large fresh orange chillies,
sliced lengthways into
julienne

ground black pepper, to taste

egg noodles with oyster mushrooms
bamee pad gab het

- Cook the noodles in boiling water for 5–6 minutes. Drain and rinse in cold water to stop further cooking.
- Heat the oil in a wok, add the garlic and give it a brief stir, then add the noodles, sugar, soy sauce, fish sauce and salt. Stir vigorously over a high heat for 1 minute.
- Add the vegetables, turn and stir continuously for 2–3 minutes, then lower the heat and check the seasoning.
- Turn on to a dish and serve at once.

khun miao's noodles

500 g/1 lb dried egg noodles

2 tablespoons plus 1 teaspoon
groundnut oil

2 garlic cloves, chopped

1½ teaspoons salt

1 teaspoon sugar

2 teaspoons vegetarian fish
sauce or soy sauce

6 dried shiitake mushrooms,
soaked, drained and sliced

125 g/4 oz tofu, diced

250 g/8 oz Chinese broccoli or
broccoli stalks, chopped
obliquely

- Cook the noodles in boiling water for 5–6 minutes. Drain and rinse in cold water to stop further cooking. Add the 2 tablespoons of groundnut oil to the noodles, mix well and set aside.
- Put the 1 teaspoon oil in a wok and heat it, then add the garlic and quickly brown it. Add all the remaining ingredients, including the noodles, and stir-fry over a high heat for 2–3 minutes.
- Turn on to a dish and serve at once.

Preparation time: 15 minutes, plus 15–20 minutes soaking
Cooking time: 10–12 minutes

Preparation time: 8 minutes
Cooking time: about 10 minutes

noodles with vegetables

pad ba mie lieung

- Cook the noodles in boiling water for 5–6 minutes. Drain and rinse in cold water to stop further cooking.
- Heat 2 tablespooons oil in a wok over a moderate heat, then add all of the ingredients one by one, including the noodles. Give a quick stir after each addition.
- Stir-fry for 3-4 minutes, adding more oil if necessary. Check the seasoning.
- Serve at once, garnished with coriander leaves.

250 g/8 oz dried egg noodles
2 tablespoons groundnut oil
50 g/2 oz leek, sliced
25 g/1 oz oyster mushrooms, torn
1 celery stalk and leaf, chopped
125 g/4 oz Chinese leaves, sliced
25 g/1 oz cauliflower florets
2 tablespoons soy sauce
1½ tablespoons sugar
½ teaspoon salt
1 teaspoon ground black pepper
2 tablespoons Crispy Garlic (see page 15)
fresh coriander leaves, to garnish

crispy noodles with vegetables

seh mee tod gab pak lohmet

- Heat the oil for deep-frying in a wok and brown the garlic. Remove with a slotted spoon and reserve.
- Put the dry noodles into the hot oil and cook until golden and crispy. Remove from the oil with a slotted spoon and drain on kitchen paper.
- Pour the oil out of the wok, leaving behind about 1 tablespoonful. Heat this oil until hot, then add all of the vegetables, the deep-fried garlic and the grated orange peel. Stir-fry for 2–3 minutes, add the fish sauce, sugar, chillies and lime juice and stir-fry again for 1 minute.
- Put the noodles in a serving dish, add the vegetables and mix them together briefly.
- Serve at once.

Preparation time: 15 minutes
Cooking time: 10 minutes

about 750 ml/1¼ pints groundnut oil for deep-frying
4 garlic cloves, chopped
125 g/4 oz dried egg noodles
1 courgette, thinly sliced
50 g/2 oz broccoli stalks, peeled and thinly sliced
50 g/2 oz onion, chopped
50 g/2 oz red pepper, chopped
50 g/2 oz mangetouts, topped, tailed and sliced obliquely
1 tablespoon grated orange peel
2 tablespoons vegetarian fish sauce or soy sauce
½ teaspoon sugar
½ teaspoon crushed dried chillies
1 tablespoon lime juice

noodles with mushrooms
pad si ew gab het laa kanah

2 tablespoons groundnut oil

375 g/12 oz dried rice sticks, soaked and drained

50 g/2 oz fresh shiitake mushrooms, finely sliced

150 g/5 oz broccoli (preferably Chinese), sliced

2 eggs, beaten

½ teaspoon sweet soy sauce (optional)

1 tablespoon sugar

½ teaspoon salt

2 tablespoons soy sauce

To serve:

1 heaped tablespoon Crispy Garlic (see page 15)

1 teaspoon ground black pepper

- Heat the oil in a wok and add the noodles. Stir-fry for 2 minutes, add the mushrooms, broccoli and eggs. Stir again, mixing the vegetables with the noodles.
- Add the sweet soy sauce (if using), the sugar, salt and soy sauce. Stir again and cook for 3–4 minutes.
- Turn on to a serving dish and sprinkle with the crispy garlic and black pepper.

Preparation time: 15 minutes, plus 15–20 minutes soaking
Cooking time: 7–8 minutes

noodles in spicy gravy *kanom jin nam prik*

1 tablespoon groundnut oil

300 g/10 oz dried rice sticks, soaked and drained

750 ml/1¼ pints Vegetable Stock (see page 19)

5 tablespoons cornflour

5 tablespoons water

150 g/5 oz broccoli

25 g/1 oz spring onions, cut into 2.5 cm/1 inch lengths

2 fresh red chillies, chopped

1½ teaspoons sugar

¼ teaspoon salt

1 teaspoon soy sauce

1 teaspoon black bean sauce

1 tablespoon Crispy Garlic (see page 15)

salt and pepper, to taste

- Heat the oil in a wok and stir-fry the noodles for 2–3 minutes until they are softened and cooked. Meanwhile, bring the stock to the boil in a saucepan.
- Mix the cornflour and water thoroughly, then add to the boiling stock, together with the broccoli and spring onions. Boil slowly and add the chillies, sugar, salt, soy sauce and black bean sauce. Stir until the gravy thickens, then add the crispy garlic and salt and pepper.
- Put the noodles into a bowl, pour the gravy over them and serve at once.

Preparation time: 15 minutes, plus 15–20 minutes soaking
Cooking time: 8–9 minutes

deep-fried noodles *mee krob*

Pickled garlic is sold in jars in oriental food shops.

- Heat the oil for deep-frying in a wok. When it is good and hot, put in a handful of the dry vermicelli. You will see it sizzle, expand and turn gold. Turn it over to ensure it is all cooked, then remove it from the oil with a slotted spoon and set aside. Continue until all the vermicelli is done.
- Slice the tofu into 2.5 cm/1 inch lengths and deep-fry until golden. Remove and set aside. Reserve the oil in the wok.
- Put the tamarind water and sugar in a separate clean wok, and stir over a moderate heat until the sugar has dissolved. Add the salt and cook for 4–5 minutes. The liquid will foam, reduce and become syrupy. Add the noodles to the syrup, then the stock, tofu and spring onion tops. Stir well over a moderate heat until well mixed.
- Turn on to a serving dish.
- Crack the egg into a small plastic bag, close it, then shake it until the egg is 'beaten'.
- Cut a corner off the bag and pour the egg in a thin stream into the hot deep-frying oil. Stir the egg around to make 'threads' and cook until golden. Remove from the oil, drain and dry on kitchen paper. Place on top of the noodles.
- Serve with the pickled garlic slices on the side, if you like.

about 750 ml/1¼ pints groundnut oil for deep-frying
150 g/5 oz dried rice vermicelli
50 g/2 oz ready-fried tofu
200 ml/7 fl oz tamarind water
6 tablespoons sugar
1 teaspoon salt
150 ml/¼ pint Vegetable Stock (see page 19)
75 g/3 oz spring onion tops
1 egg
2–3 bulbs pickled garlic, sliced (optional), to serve

Preparation time: 10 minutes
Cooking time: 25 minutes

chilli fried noodles *kwetio kua*

- Heat the oil in a wok. Crack the eggs into it and stir them around, then add the crispy garlic and shallots and stir-fry for 30 seconds. Add the noodles and stir-fry briefly, then add the rest of the ingredients. Stir-fry vigorously for 2–3 minutes.
- Turn on to a dish and serve at once.

1 tablespoon groundnut oil
2 eggs
2 tablespoons Crispy Garlic and Shallots (see page 15)
325 g/11 oz dried wide rice noodles, soaked and drained
2 tablespoons sugar
1½ tablespoons soy sauce
50 g/2 oz asparagus spears, cut into 2.5 cm/1 inch lengths
1 celery stalk, finely chopped
2 spring onions, finely chopped
1 teaspoon ground black pepper
1 tablespoon crushed dried chillies
salt, to taste

Preparation time: 15 minutes, plus 15–20 minutes soaking
Cooking time: 6 minutes

pickles and *dipping sauces*

Snacks and salads in Thailand are usually accompanied by one or two dipping sauces, and a dish of pickles often appears on the table too. There is generally a sour sharp sauce, such as soy and vinegar, and a sweet one, such as plum. The aim is to achieve a good contrast of tastes, so a sweetish snack such as stuffed cucumber benefits from a sharp dipping sauce. Pickles are widely used, again as a contrast to the other flavours in the meal. They are very simple to make and last well, so it is worth making more than you need and keeping the extra in the refrigerator.

4 eggs, in their shells
1.2 litres/2 pints water
100 g/4 oz salt

Preparation time: 10 minutes, plus about 1 hour cooling and 15 days standing
Cooking time: 10 minutes

salted eggs
kai kem

- Heat the water in a saucepan and dissolve the salt in it. Remove from the heat and allow to cool.
- When the water is cool, pour it into a jar and gently add the whole eggs. Put the lid on and allow to stand at room temperature for 15 days.
- Remove the eggs from the jar and hard-boil.

rice water pickle

- Bring the water to the boil in a large saucepan, add the rice and continue to boil for 15 minutes. Meanwhile, peel the mooli and carrots and slice them thinly, and cut the Chinese leaves into 2.5 cm/1 inch slices. Pat the vegetables dry with kitchen paper and set aside.
- Strain the water off the rice into a bowl, then set the water aside to cool. Discard the rice.
- Take a 2.4 litre/4 pint jar and fill it with layers of vegetables, sprinkling garlic, ginger, peppercorns and salt between each layer and ending with a sprinkling of salt on top. Bury the whole shallot and the whole chillies in the middle.
- Add the cooled rice water to just cover the top layer, cover the jar with muslin and let it stand in a cool place for 4 days, making sure the level of the liquid does not drop. If it does, top it up with cold water.
- The pickle will be ready to eat after 4 days, and you can put the lid on the jar and keep it in the refrigerator, where the pickle will keep for several weeks.

2 litres/4 pints water
250 g/8 oz glutinous rice
1 mooli radish
2 carrots
375 g/12 oz Chinese leaves or cabbage
3 garlic cloves, thinly sliced
1 tablespoon peeled and thinly sliced fresh root ginger
1 teaspoon black peppercorns
2 tablespoons salt
1 shallot, peeled
2 large fresh chillies (preferably red and yellow)

Preparation time: 25 minutes, plus cooling and 4 days standing
Cooking time: 25 minutes

pickled cucumber and carrot

75 ml/3 fl oz distilled white
vinegar or Chinese
rice vinegar

3 teaspoons caster sugar

½ teaspoon salt

½ cucumber, peeled, deseeded
and chopped

¼ carrot, chopped lengthways
into julienne

1 shallot, finely chopped

1 small fresh red chilli, finely
chopped

○ Put all the ingredients in an airtight jar and shake until well mixed. Leave to stand at room temperature for 2 hours.

○ Remove the lid, pour into a bowl and serve.

pickled ginger

125 g/4 oz fresh root ginger

¼ teaspoon salt

125 ml/4 fl oz rice vinegar

1 tablespoon caster sugar

○ Peel the ginger and cut it into the thinnest possible slices. Leave it to stand in a bowl of cold water for 30 minutes.

○ Boil a saucepan of water. Remove the ginger from the bowl of cold water with a slotted spoon and drop it into the boiling water. Bring back to a brisk boil over a high heat, drain and allow to cool.

○ Spread the ginger out on a plate and sprinkle with salt. In a small saucepan, combine the vinegar and sugar and heat until the sugar has fully dissolved. Place the ginger in a jar and pour the mixture over it, mixing thoroughly. Allow to cool, then put the top on the jar and place it in the refrigerator.

○ The pickled ginger will turn a very pale pink colour, and will be ready to use after 1 week. It will keep in the refrigerator for 3–4 months.

Preparation time: 40 minutes, plus 30 minutes and 1 week standing
Cooking time: 18–20 minutes

plum sauce

5 tablespoons distilled white
vinegar or Chinese rice
vinegar
4 tablespoons plum jam
I small fresh red chilli, finely
sliced

O Put the vinegar and jam in a small saucepan and heat gently, mixing thoroughly.
O Remove from the heat, turn into a small bowl and allow to cool.
O Add the sliced fresh chilli before serving.

Preparation time: I minute
Cooking time: 2 minutes

sweet nut sauce

75 ml/3 fl oz distilled
white vinegar or Chinese
rice vinegar
60 g/2½ oz palm sugar or light
muscovado sugar
I teaspoon salt
½ teaspoon crushed dried
chillies
2½ tablespoons Crushed
Roasted Peanuts (see
page 16)
fresh coriander leaves, to
garnish

O Heat the vinegar, sugar and salt in a saucepan until the sugar has dissolved and the liquid thickens a little. Remove from the heat, add the chillies and peanuts and then mix well.
O Turn the sauce into a bowl and garnish with coriander leaves.

Preparation time: 2 minutes
Cooking time: 2 minutes

hot sweet sauce

100 ml/3½ fl oz distilled
white vinegar or Chinese
rice vinegar
60 g/2½ oz palm sugar or light
muscovado sugar
¼ teaspoon salt
I small fresh green chilli, finely
chopped
I small fresh red chilli, finely
chopped

O Pour the vinegar into a small saucepan and place over a gentle heat. Add the sugar and salt and cook, stirring, until the sugar has dissolved. Remove from the heat and allow to cool.
O Pour the sauce into a small bowl and add the chopped fresh chillies.

Preparation time: I minute
Cooking time: 1–2 minutes

1 heaped teaspoon Red Curry Paste (see page 12)

1 tablespoon groundnut oil

250 ml/8 fl oz coconut milk

50 g/2 oz sugar

25 ml/1 fl oz vegetarian fish sauce or soy sauce

juice of 1 lime

65 g/2½ oz Crushed Roasted Peanuts (see page 16)

1 teaspoon crushed dried chillies

Preparation time: 3–4 minutes
Cooking time: 3–5 minutes

satay sauce

○ Put the curry paste in a saucepan with the oil and stir over a gentle heat for 1 minute. Add the rest of the ingredients and then cook over a moderate heat until thickened and amalgamated. Remove the pan from the heat, turn into a bowl and allow to cool.

soy and vinegar dipping sauce

○ Combine all the ingredients in a bowl and stir until the sugar has dissolved.

Preparation time: 2 minutes

3 tablespoons distilled white vinegar or Chinese rice vinegar

3 tablespoons dark soy sauce

1½ teaspoons caster sugar

2 small fresh red chillies, finely sliced

Fruit is one of Thailand's major exports, and deservedly so. The range of fruit is enormous, and even though the fruits are seasonal, the next variety is always ready to come along. Pineapples and coconuts are available all year round. Mangoes, which along with those from Pakistan and West Africa rate amongst the world's best, are seasonal in Thailand – but not, of course, in our supermarkets where we can always find mangoes from some part of the world. There are delicate mangosteen, star fruit, sapodilla, jack fruit, strawberries and too many more to mention. Thai fruit drinks are delicious, and it is easy to whizz up a thirst-quencher or an exotic cocktail for summer days or nights. Children who have to be cajoled into eating fruit seem to have no problem drinking it. Thais eat fruit at the end of a meal rather than dessert, which they eat at any time of day as a sweet snack.

desserts
and
drinks

2 ripe mangoes
1 small ripe papaya
250 g/8 oz lychees
1 slice of watermelon
1 lime, cut into quarters

Preparation time: 15–20 minutes

fresh fruit platter

- ○ Peel and thickly slice the mangoes and cut the papaya into four or eight. Peel the lychees. Cut the watermelon into chunks, removing as many of the seeds as you can.
- ○ Arrange the fruit on a serving plate, with the lime quarters ready to squeeze over the papaya.

chatuchak mocktail

300 ml/½ pint coconut milk
450 ml/¾ pint pineapple juice
1 banana, peeled and sliced
250 ml/8 fl oz soda water
ice, to serve

- ○ Put all the ingredients, except the ice, in a blender and blend until smooth.
- ○ Serve over ice, in tall glasses.

Preparation time: 2 minutes

625 g/1¼ lb pumpkin
1.2 litres/2 pints coconut milk
200 g/7 oz palm sugar or light muscovado sugar
75 g/3 oz sugar
1 teaspoon salt

Preparation time: 15 minutes
Cooking time: 15 minutes

pumpkin in coconut cream

- Peel the pumpkin with a vegetable scraper, leaving some of the skin still in place. This helps the pumpkin pieces remain intact during cooking and improves the texture of the dish. Cut the pumpkin into 1 cm/½ inch dice.
- Pour the coconut milk into a saucepan, add the sugar and salt and stir until the sugar has dissolved and the liquid is smooth. Add the pumpkin and bring slowly to the boil, stirring. Lower the heat and simmer, stirring as the coconut milk thickens, for 10 minutes or until the pumpkin pieces are softened.
- Serve hot.

Makes 12
Preparation time: 15 minutes, plus 1½ hours cooling and setting
Cooking time: 20 minutes

coconut balls

maprow geow

300 ml/½ pint water
300 g/10 oz sugar
250 g/8 oz grated fresh
   coconut or desiccated
   coconut softened with a little
   cold water

In Thailand, food colouring is often put into this mixture to jazz up the appearance a little. Yellow and pink are popular colours to use.

- Boil the water and sugar to make a thick sugar syrup. Add the coconut and continue boiling until the syrup has almost all evaporated.
- Put 12 tablespoonfuls of the mixture on a metal baking tray, shaping each spoonful into a ball as you go.
- Allow to cool and harden for about 1½ hours.

coconut cream custard *sang kia*

maprow on

2 large eggs
200 ml/7 fl oz coconut milk
175 g/6 oz palm sugar or light
   muscovado sugar
¼ teaspoon salt
2 banana leaves (optional)

- Beat the eggs together in a bowl and add the coconut milk and sugar. Mix well, add the salt and mix again.
- You can pour this mixture into 4 ramekins or, if you prefer, into banana leaf bowls.
- To make banana leaf bowls, cut 8 equal-size circles from the banana leaves and place 2 pieces together, shiny side out. Make 4 pleats opposite each other, and secure with toothpicks to form a bowl. Make 3 more bowls in the same way.
- Put the filled ramekins or banana leaf bowls in a steamer and steam for 15–20 minutes. Serve warm, on a plate.

Preparation time: 5 minutes
Cooking time: 15–20 minutes

Preparation time: 10 minutes, plus 6–8 hours soaking and 30 minutes standing
Cooking time: 30 minutes

mango and sticky rice *kaoniao mamuang*

500 g/1 lb glutinous rice, soaked for at least 6 hours or overnight
150 g/5 oz sugar
300 ml/½ pint coconut milk
2 ripe mangoes

- Drain and rinse the rice well. Cook in a steamer for about 30 minutes. Give the rice a good shake halfway through steaming to ensure it is evenly cooked.
- While the rice is steaming, combine the sugar and coconut milk in a large bowl and stir well.
- When the rice is cooked, transfer it to the coconut mixture and stir thoroughly for 2–3 minutes to achieve a rather creamy consistency. Cover with a lid and allow to stand at room temperature for 30 minutes.
- Before serving, slice the mangoes and arrange them attractively on a dish around the rice.

watermelon sorbet

500 g/1 lb watermelon, skin removed, deseeded and chopped
200 g/7 oz caster sugar
250 ml/8 fl oz water
2 cinnamon sticks
40 ml/1½ fl oz lime juice
1 egg white

- Put the watermelon in a heavy-bottomed saucepan over a low heat. Cook gently until it becomes soft.
- In a separate saucepan, dissolve the sugar in the water and add the cinnamon sticks. Bring to the boil and cook for 5 minutes, then remove from the heat. Cover the pan and leave the syrup to cool and infuse.
- Strain the syrup into the watermelon purée and stir in the lime juice. Pour the mixture into a freezer container, cover and freeze for 2 hours, removing it at 30 minute intervals and beating it with a fork to ensure no ice crystals form.
- Beat the egg white until stiff and add it to the mixture, blending it in thoroughly.
- Freeze for 1 hour, beating once with a fork after 30 minutes. Transfer the mixture to the refrigerator 30 minutes before serving.
- Serve individual scoops in bowls.

Preparation time: 10 minutes, plus 3 hours freezing
Cooking time: 12–15 minutes

Preparation time: 8 minutes
Cooking time: 10 minutes

about 750 ml/1¼ pints
  groundnut oil for deep-frying
750 g/1½ lb bananas or small
  plantains
caster sugar, to serve

Batter:
190 ml/6½ fl oz water
150 g/5 oz rice flour or plain
  flour
125 g/4 oz freshly grated or
  desiccated coconut
½ teaspoon salt
75 g/3 oz sugar
1 egg

banana fritters
kwai kek

- First make the batter: put the water, flour, coconut, salt, sugar and egg in a bowl and mix together.
- Heat the oil for deep-frying in a wok. While it is heating, peel the bananas, cut each one into thirds lengthways, then cut each third crossways to make slices about 7 cm/3 inches long.
- Coat the banana slices with the batter and then drop them carefully into the hot oil, 3–4 at a time. Cook the banana over a moderate heat for 3–4 minutes until golden brown. Remove the fritters from the oil with a slotted spoon and drain on kitchen paper.
- When all the slices are cooked, arrange them on a serving dish and sprinkle with caster sugar. Serve at once.

pradiphat papaya

375 g/12 oz ripe papaya,
  peeled and sliced
175 ml/6 fl oz white rum
250 ml/8 fl oz pineapple juice
75 ml/3 fl oz lime or lemon
  juice
75 ml/3 fl oz sugar syrup
6 ice cubes, crushed
fresh mint leaves, to decorate

To make sugar syrup, heat 250 g/8 oz sugar with 300 ml/½ pint water until the sugar has dissolved. Allow to cool before using.

- Put all the ingredients in a blender and blend until the ice is crushed.
- Serve in tall glasses, decorated with mint leaves.

Preparation time: 8–10 minutes

2 ripe mangoes, peeled and sliced

125 ml/4 fl oz tequila

50 ml/2 fl oz Triple Sec

25 ml/1 fl oz grenadine

75 ml/3 fl oz lime or lemon juice

75 ml/3 fl oz sugar syrup

6 ice cubes, crushed

lime or lemon slices, to serve

Preparation time: 10–12 minutes

silom sunrise

○ Put all the ingredients in a blender and blend until the ice is crushed.

○ Serve in pretty glasses, with lime or lemon slices.

siamese slammer

125 ml/4 fl oz vodka

juice of 2 oranges

1 small ripe papaya, peeled and chopped

1 banana, peeled and sliced

juice of 1 lime

125 ml/4 fl oz sugar syrup (see page 122)

ice

○ Put all the ingredients in a blender and blend until smooth.

Preparation time: 5 minutes

index